Thanks for
making the s
happen! :)

Road to Wonder:
Finding the Extra in Your Ordinary

To Teri
Keep chasing
wonder!

Road to Wonder

Finding the Extra in Your Ordinary

Taylor Hughes

Road to Wonder: Finding the Extra in Your Ordinary

Published in Upland, CA, by WonderFull Entertainment.

Editor: Jamie Chavez
Typesetter: Paul Salvette
Cover Design: ebooklaunch.com
Author Photo: Taylor Wong

ISBN # 978-0-578-95620-6

Printed in the United States of America

For my high school sweetheart, Katie, and our two amazing girls, Maddy and Kenz.

I love chasing wonder with you.

Table of Contents

Foreword by Bob Goff

I'M NOT A jigsaw puzzle guy. If you are, we can still be friends, but just barely. Activity is my vice. I talk fast, I work fast, I think fast and I eat fast—I make coffee nervous. Whether you resonate with this way of living or react to it, we still all have a lot in common. If you are like the rest of us, you are trying to figure out your life. My guess is that you want what I want, and what almost everybody wants: love, purpose, connection, and a few authentic relationships. Your list might be longer than this, but I'm pretty sure if you keep it real, it won't be any shorter. So what is getting in the way of us pursuing what matters to us the most?

If I were going to solve this problem like it was a jig-saw puzzle, I would find the four corners first and start there. My first corner would be my faith. Everyone has beliefs. You may believe that life is fundamentally fair or that it is incredibly unfair. You may believe people are generally good, even though you have met a couple bad ones. You may believe in God, or you may be believe in none of the above. My faith is what I am hoping will help me connect all the other sometimes disconnected pieces in my life together.

Two other corners in my life I would find first would

be my family and my friends. These are the evergreen relationships in my life that fill it with beauty and make my life work. When I have a right perspective and I show up for these two important areas of my life, I feel more grounded, more well-anchored for the storms life sometimes sends our way.

The final corner in my life puzzle is something my longtime friend Taylor has taught me—and it's the power of wonder in our lives. Wonder isn't something we sign up for, it's something we lean in to. We collect it, then distribute it. We are rivers, not reservoirs. We are not wonder's advocates, we are merely its messengers. And if we are willing to do the difficult work of surrounding our lives with it, like the edge pieces of the puzzle, the rest of the puzzle pieces will find their places.

We don't need instructions for our lives, we need examples. This book and the stories Taylor tells in it are the picture on the puzzle box. They show us what a life of purpose and joy and wonder look like, and invite us to figure out where the rest of the pieces we hold in our hands fit in.

I am honored to introduce to you to my dear friend, teacher, and the wonder-maker, Taylor Hughes.

Introduction: What Happened to Wonder?

SOMETHING HAS GONE missing—and most of us have not even noticed. Unlike when you lose your car keys or glasses and begin a hurried search, no one is panicking to recover this lost treasure. It is a thing that was not earned or purchased and yet its value is irreplaceable. Without it there can be no true discovery, no revolution. Old as time itself, this forgotten gift is the key that those who came before us used to unlock the great mysteries, and we now take for granted. I am talking about *wonder*.

Do you remember wonder? There used to be a time that we didn't know everything. Before we carried supercomputers in our pockets, before search engines gave us immediate access to answers, we had to search elsewhere. We would sit alone in our favorite chair or lie on a blanket stargazing with friends, and we would wonder. Without the stress of deadlines and clocks, we allowed ourselves to journey to another place. A place of endless possibilities where new discoveries were made.

I am not talking about returning to ignorance. This is not like that guy in *The Matrix* who says, "Put me back in!" I'm also not trying to suggest that we need to go back to the good ol' days—a statement often made by people who have not studied history enough to know that those days were not all that great to begin with. This is a simple challenge to get back to a place of possibilities. A place where we look at our life, our families, our work, and wonder . . . *What if I actually pursued that dream? What if we said yes to that crazy idea our kids have?*

As long as I can remember, I have been obsessed with moments of wonder. Moments that remind us that there is something more out there. The feeling you get on Christmas morning, or on your first trip to Disneyland, or seeing a really good magic show. There is something incredible about being in a place that reminds you that you don't have it all figured out. What if we could stay in a place of awe regardless of our current situation? To realize that the lives we call ordinary already contain the extra we are looking for? We just need to open ourselves back up to wonder.

In the pages that follow you'll read true and personal moments from my life. I don't for a second want to infer that my story is any more special than yours. In fact, my desire is that you will see the power of *every person's story.* I hope you are entertained along the way, but most importantly I hope you are encouraged to see the wonder that exists all around you.

The Magic Milk Pitcher

IT WAS THE morning of my seventh birthday and all my friends from school sat crisscross applesauce awaiting the surprise my parents had planned. I grew up in a house that was the perfect setting for a good mystery. Built in 1901, it had lived almost an entire lifetime before I was brought home from the hospital. My favorite feature was the two large pocket doors that separated the living room from the dining room—the kind of doors that when they opened seemed to vanish into the walls. It was behind these very doors that my parents had staged my big birthday surprise.

My folks slowly pulled the two panels apart like they were drawing back the curtains for a Broadway show on opening night. And standing there, in my living room was, of all things, a magician. I sat there, mouth gaped, staring in amazement. I had never seen a magic show in person before, and although it wasn't Christmas morning, it felt the same. The gentleman performer presented one amazing trick after another. Silks appeared from his fingertips. A chosen card was lost then found, and then he presented something that to this day is one of the most miraculous things I have ever seen.

The magician took a single sheet of newspaper, folded it into a makeshift funnel and proceeded to pour a pitcher of milk into the newly formed cone. Once the vessel had been filled to the brim, he waved his hand and a moment later, the newspaper unrolled revealing that the milk had vanished. All of a sudden, at seven years old, my life had purpose. Not only was I committed to learning the trick, but I had a vision of myself performing it to a standing ovation of my peers.

My first step in search of the secret was to ask the magician. After all, he clearly knew how the trick was done. I was certain he would recognize that I had what it took, invite me to be his apprentice, and also tell me how he shoved that bird in his pocket. I don't know how much you know about the magi, but one thing they aren't too keen on is revealing their trade secrets to seven-year-olds.

The next day I begged my mom to take me to the local library, where I discovered section 793.8 of the Dewey Decimal System. This is the place where they keep all the magic books at every library in America! It was on this shelf that I discovered books containing the secrets to many of magic's great mysteries: How to vanish a coin. How to levitate a dollar bill. There was even a book on a magician's most impossible feat—how to impress women with card tricks. Really.

Finally, in an old catalogue for a company called Owen Magic Supreme, I found the answer I was looking for. Owen had built many props for the great magicians of the day, like David Copperfield and Lance Burton. Sure, enough item #4152 in the catalogue was "The Magic Milk Pitcher." It was then that I realized the secret was the special pitcher itself. There was no mystical incantation, no special magic words passed down from shaman to warlock to birthday party clown. It was simply a trick pitcher and if I had the pitcher, I, too, could be the magician.

The only downside was the price tag of $375! To a seven-year-old that might as well have been a million. I spent the next three years performing simple magic with things I found around the house and was able to impress my family and friends. In fact, I was even able to book my first paying gig performing for my friend Shannon's tenth birthday. Her dad offered to pay me twenty-five dollars and all the pizza I could eat. I couldn't shake his hand fast enough.

I rehearsed for weeks leading up to the big day but wasn't sure how to end the show. The day before the performance I walked into the local magic shop I frequented and immediately noticed something I had not seen before. There on the dusty old shelf behind the counter sat item #4152 from the Owen Magic Supreme Catalogue. The Magic Milk Pitcher!

Apparently, an older magician had retired and was selling off his collection. The best part was they only wanted fifteen dollars for the pitcher! I bought the pitcher, ran home to practice and it worked beautifully. I could not wait to perform the trick at the party. The next day everyone was seated in front of the gazebo while I successfully practiced the milk pitcher once more before showtime. The whole show went smoothly, and it was time for the big finish.

In an effort to build up to the finale, I invited Shannon

in her new blue satin birthday dress to join me on stage and take a seat. I formed the newspaper into a cone in my left hand, then grabbed the pitcher with my right hand just as I remembered the magician doing at my party. I held up the pitcher, I held up the cone. Then in a moment of pure genius or madness, I held them both up over Shannon's head. As I began to pour I couldn't remember if I had reset the pitcher after my last rehearsal.

Without revealing too much, the pitcher needed to be reset after every performance—because the first time you pour magic happens and the second time you pour milk happens. I mistakenly poured an entire half gallon of milk all over my friend Shannon. Pandemonium swept through the backyard. Everyone screamed. Everyone, that is, except my friend Cody, who had just chugged a Capri Sun and did a huge spit take all over the front row. Then it got dead quiet as everyone looked at poor Shannon covered in milk. She looked at herself, then me, and then she did one of the kindest things possible . . . she laughed.

I learned that day from Shannon the freedom that comes from not taking yourself too seriously. If she hadn't laughed, if it had ruined her party, I can almost guarantee you that I would have retired from magic right then. The fact that she realized at age ten that if it is going to be funny later, it's OK to laugh about it now was extraordinary—and everyone who was there still remembers that moment with fondness.

Extra

I AM NOT saying you should be reckless in your pursuits. Whatever you do you should give it your all. I have just found that one of the ways to find the extra in your ordinary life is to take what you do seriously, but never take yourself so seriously. Admittedly this is easier said than done. On more occasions than I would like to admit I have found myself so worried about a mistake I made that I have been unable to move past it. Have you ever been there?

I wonder what would happen if we chose to take responsibility for our mistakes without being defined by them. If we could remember that every great success came after a long timeline of ups and downs. If we gave ourselves the same forgiveness we try to give to others. I believe if we did, life would be a little more magical.

Basketball and Buried Treasure

MOVIES WERE MY babysitter as a kid. That sounds a little weird to say but for a ten-year-old whose mom had no other choice than to work following my parents' divorce, it was a pretty fantastic arrangement. And while our neighborhood certainly contained a few "latch-key" kids, I thought of myself as a "TV remote" kid. My sister was two years older and technically of the age that she could look after me. So after school I would come home and make myself a snack, usually a Hot Pocket or micro-waved hot dog. I would then push the big orange button that caused the top of our VCR to open like a New York sidewalk cellar, settle into my red beanbag chair, and disappear into one of the films I had seen several dozen times.

Somehow they always felt brand new. The beautiful thing about movies like *The Goonies* or *Stand by Me* is they show young people going on these amazing journeys. Being of a similar age, I looked at all of these adventures as possibilities that could *actually happen*. I wanted to have a legitimate adventure like I saw in the movies—a no-parental-supervision, semi-illegal, lifelong-memory kind of adventure, with a rousing, uplifting musical score to boot!

Who would have thought that a lack of funding for our city park would create an incredible place for an adventure to happen? I grew up in Azusa, California, whose motto was "Everything from A to Z in the USA." To be perfectly frank, it took me a few years to realize it spelled out "AZUSA" ... I'm sure you can probably guess my grade point average in those days. As a kid, I never understood this motto because it seemed like our city didn't have much of *anything* other than a community pool and a basketball court. Both of these were located at the park right across the street from my house. This is the same park where I was in my only ever fistfight. It was a one-punch, but not because the bully fell when I hit him. It was because I ran away immediately after taking a swing. This was also when I found out that if you live across the street from where the fight occurs, you have to keep running past your house so he doesn't know where to find you later.

The summer after I turned ten the city pulled out the basketball courts in order to install new hoops, then ran out of money—leaving a dirt lot with massive trenches where the old hoops were removed. For the many kids in our neighborhood who loved sports this was devastating, but for a kid looking for adventure it was the perfect setup.

I loaded up an old army footlocker I got on a trip to the surplus store with my dad. In it was a large camouflage net and my most prized possessions: three 1950s-era cap guns. These were toy guns that looked real. Not plastic—they were die-cast metal. My pops had given then to me and as a kid I thought they were amazing.

That entire summer I—along with my next-door

neighbor and a few other friends—created the most amazing and elaborate forts out of those ditches at the park. We used shovels to make trenches, the camouflage netting became the roof, and each day we added to our stockpile of supplies. We played a game called Bigger or Better, breaking into teams and going door to door, trading with neighbors for larger items—starting with a penny. We collected old tires, tarps, anything we could use for a fort. Albert was the ultimate winner, hauling in a small battery-operated TV so we could watch cartoons in the bunker.

Eventually we got tired of bringing all the supplies to the park each day, so we would load the valuable supplies in the footlocker and hide it behind rocks in a small alcove we'd made. The next morning we would uncover it and set up our base camp. It was the perfect security plan.

One Monday morning in August, I heard strange noise. It wasn't the ice cream truck I had grown accustomed to hearing every morning living by the park. Oh no, this was a much louder sound. I opened the balcony door of my bedroom that overlooked the park, and I couldn't believe what I saw.

It was a cement mixer! Apparently the city had found the funds to continue the project and they began by setting the huge concrete hoops in our fort and surrounding them with cement.

I ran across the street in my pajamas and stared at that concrete pool that was now covering my childhood. To say that I was devastated would be an understatement. I had just lost my favorite belongings—and a place

I'd created and loved but would never be able to visit again. I spent the next few weeks in a funk not knowing if I would ever get over it. Then I began to wonder.

Extra

WONDER MOVES US beyond the moment we are stuck in. It allows us to see things from a different perspective and find the extra in these ordinary moments. I realized that every great adventure movie I loved started with a loss. If One-Eyed Willie had never lost his treasure, the Goonies couldn't have discovered it. I started to imagine that one day perhaps fifty years from now, the city would decide it was once again time to rebuild the park, and under that old concrete they would find a time capsule, a monument to the greatest summer of my childhood.

Maybe you have lost something more significant. A job, a relationship, a dream you believed in is gone. I wonder what would happen if we chose to honor the past but not live in it. To be grateful for our memories and experiences but to press forward and create some new ones. To navigate any map, you have to first know where you are. Recognizing your starting point is an important part of the process, but it is just the first step. No matter what challenges led to the place you are currently in, remember the journey isn't over. There is a treasure chest of extraordinary adventures waiting for you. You just have to keep going.

Making Things Happen

WHEN I WAS a kid I was obsessed with prop making. My best buddy, Cody, and I couldn't decide whether we would be magicians someday or special-effects artists for the movies. We recently reconnected after many years apart, and it was fantastic to see that he went into special effects while I work primarily as a magician. As kids, though, we spent a couple years absolutely obsessed with recreating props from the movies of our day. Whether it was the idol from *Raiders of the Lost Ark*, the sword from *The Princess Bride*, or levitating hoverboards from *Back to the Future* that we tried to sell to our fellow classmates . . . we just built it.

This passion for building led to a low inventory of essential supplies at home. My always supportive mom would often give me several six packs of Scotch tape in my Christmas stocking or wonder where that whole roll of aluminum foil she'd just bought had gone to. I knew exactly what happened to it. It takes a lot of foil to build the laser from *Honey, I Shrunk the Kids*. I am so grateful that my parents didn't find this annoying or weird, even though I know at times it was both. They always encouraged me that if I wanted to build something, use what I had and build it.

In a strange parallel, my wife grew up in a household where her father could do anything. He never once called a repair person. Whether it was repairing their computer or rebuilding a transmission, he fixed it himself. More than that, he instilled in Katie and her siblings that they could do the same. When it comes to taking on projects, my wife is fearless. Katie was instilled with the confidence that if you don't know how to do it, you can figure it out. We are both so grateful to have had supportive parents and are very intentional in our approach with our own daughters. By the time our girls were ten years old, they were cooking full meals and using power tools. But not at the same time.

Perhaps you are reading this and you didn't grow up in a supportive environment; perhaps your family made you feel incapable. I am here to tell you that you are fully capable of building the life you want to have. "I don't know how" is an excuse I feel like we should all omit from our vocabulary. We live in a time where we have instant access to all human knowledge. If you don't know how to do something, not only is there someone else who does know, but chances are they have already filmed, edited, and uploaded a tutorial on YouTube that will walk you through it step by step. The biggest thing holding you back isn't a lack of resources, it is a lack of action. Just go! Give yourself permission and start doing the thing today!

For years I wanted to have my own TV show. An hour of magic, storytelling, and comedy recorded before a live audience. I still remember the feel of the carpet in my grandparents' living room as I lay there in anticipation about to watch David Copperfield perform one mystery after another. It was more than a magic show— he told stories and made you feel like anything was possible. A few years later I saw Harry Anderson, an amazing magician and actor known for his portrayal of the judge on the TV show *Night Court*. His comedy-magic TV special *Hello, Sucker!* sealed the deal for me. I told myself, *Someday I want to do that*. This word *someday* is the killer of many a great work of art. *Someday* lives in the world of intentions, but we need to take action on our dreams today. I was five when *Hello, Sucker!* came out and thirty-three years later I was still saying, "Someday, I want to make a show like that."

The funny thing is by this time I had started performing regularly at the Comedy and Magic Club in Hermosa Beach, California. This was the very same venue where Harry recorded his iconic special. Every time I stood on that stage to perform I thought, "I really should get around to making my magic-and-comedy special." It took just one breakfast with a very bold friend to kick me out of *someday* into action.

It was August of 2019 in Nashville, Tennessee. I was just starting a week of shows at a great little theater and nightclub called House of Cards. Our friends Vance and Chelsea live in Atlanta but just happened to be visiting Nashville at the same time and met me for breakfast the next morning. That day Vance asked me a question that still echoes in my head: "What is something you know you need to do but haven't done?"

I knew just the answer.

Without skipping a beat, I jumped into my pitch of the special, and I painted a great picture. After all, I had been thinking about doing this for more than thirty years! When I got to the crescendo of what this show could look like, Vance interrupted me and in the kindest, most direct way and said, "Bro, you told me this same idea last year . . . so when are you going to do it?" I immediately went into excuse mode, saying I was too busy with travel, and so on. Vance then took out his phone and asked me when the next free week I had on my calendar was. I looked and said, "Well, I guess the first week of January." He said, "Done." He then booked a plane ticket and said he would fly out that week and help me with whatever I needed to insure I didn't back out.

It was because I made a commitment to a date and to Vance that the special got made. Granted, I had never made a TV show and didn't know what to do—but that didn't matter. I put a date on the calendar and that got the ball rolling. What I found out next was that the details started to line up. It was a ton of work, a ton of money, and a lot of stress, but it was also wonderful. If Vance hadn't booked that flight, I might be still talking about *someday*, but because we both took *action*, it is now ten months later and I have my own comedy magic special available on a major platform.

Extra

WHATEVER IT IS you need to do, no matter how big or small, the first step is always getting started. Whether you want to change a garbage disposal or write a screenplay, there are helpful people and resources within reach. You just have to make the commitment to action and then take the first step. I encourage you right now to speak life into your someday project and put a deadline on the calendar. The very thought might bring you anxiety . . . and that is OK. Use it for fuel and just go.

The Ride Is More Important than the Destination

I CAN STILL smell the original interior, feel the way the seat rumbled beneath us as we cruised down every back alley in my childhood neighborhood. As a kid, there was nothing better than riding in my dad's 1954 Chevrolet. It was the early 1980s but you would never hear Duran Duran or Bon Jovi coming through this radio. My dad is old school all the way, so while everyone else was cranking "Papa don't preach," my dad was sharing the good news about the Supremes, Dick Dale, and Chuck Berry.

It didn't matter where we were headed, the first stop was always the same. "The Little Pepsi in the Bottle Store" was not its real name; in fact, I don't know the actual name of this little market that was just a few blocks from the house. All I knew is that they sold little glass bottles of Pepsi which at the time were a rare treat. The only places they seemed to have them were at this little market or if you took a trip down to Mexico.

I can't tell you why it tasted better out of the bottle or how it seemed so much colder than when you bought it in a can. What I can tell you is that nothing made me feel more like a grown-up than sitting with my dad in the front seat of his Chevy drinking out of a glass bottle. There was no air conditioning, and even if there had been my dad wouldn't use it. He called his AC a two-fifty-five: two windows rolled down while you drove fifty-five miles an hour. He would rest his elbow on the window frame and could grab the top of the window with his left hand. I measured my growth as a child by how far my hand was from the top when I tried to mimic him. It was my greatest aspiration to be able to do this. If you tried to drink your soda while driving he would make a joke by tapping on the brakes before smiling with his eyes and reminding you to only take a drink when the driver did.

We had a road near our house that we call the roller-coaster road. I later learned that it was called Sierra Madre but when you rode with Dad, everything had a nickname. This road had the biggest dip and the only thing that came close was the drop on Pirates of the Caribbean at Disneyland. There were signs warning you to slow down at a certain point, but my dad figured out if you gun it at that sign you could get airborne when you went back up the other side. Your stomach would fly up into your throat and because there were no seat belts in his car you would often make contact with the ceiling before landing back on the seat. This was very unsafe, terrifying, and one of my favorite things about my childhood. I am happy to have experienced this at least a hundred times before they ruined the road by fixing it a few years ago.

We rarely rode on the freeway, not because we couldn't but because my dad loves the ride. Remember, we were cruising. When you rode in the Chevy there were no curfews and no time deadlines. We got there when we got there. We took every side street, backroad, and alley we could find. We discovered parks I never knew about and would often pull over to check out a yard sale or just to climb a tree for no other reason than it looked like it needed to be climbed. We lived about an hour from the beach but would often take two hours or more to get there because we decided to have an adventure along the way. I learned from my dad that these things were not distractions or delays keeping us from our destination. Often the best stories and memories were made because of these interruptions to our plans.

As I recall these moments with my dad, I am realizing for the first time that his way of being can be summarized with one phrase: *The ride is more important than the destination.*

Very often when we were having a bad day or were bored my dad would just say, "Let's go for a cruise." I think if many of us tried that today the response we might receive would be, "Where are we going?" Or, "Why are we gonna do that?" For my dad, that is never a concern. Ultimately we are gonna end up where the road takes us; we can't control everything that happens but we can choose to enjoy the journey. I don't want to make it sound like my dad is carefree or has lived the easy life; he has challenges like all of us, but he has chosen to not let those challenges keep him from enjoying every day.

Extra

WHEN I FIRST jotted down this memory I didn't have a "lesson" in mind, but it challenged me to find one. To be perfectly honest, there have been quite a few times in my life when I have been so worried about where I was going that I had forgotten to enjoy the journey. I have spent many hours and lots of money on books, therapy, and meditation. All of which I believe in and am grateful for—and yet I realized that all of these things have been trying to get me to simply be present the way my dad is every day.

I'm still learning how to reset my mind to approach life this way. And I may never be able to fully possess this glorious default that my dad switches to with ease. But I do know what my first steps are—step away from the computer, call my dad to thank him, put the kids in the car, throw on some oldies, and find a road we have never driven down before. My hope for you is that on your way to wherever you're going today, you will find a wonderful interruption to your plans that you will remember for years to come.

Brick and Mortar Magic

As I HAVE mentioned, my obsession with magic started early. It's how I learned what a phone book was. (Some of you reading this might be learning what a phone book is right now.) Long before the Internet gave us the power to find, research, and receive directions from a disembodied voice to a particular business, if you needed to find a plumber, nail salon, or pet store, you looked it up in the local phone book. As soon as I realized that magic shops put ads in the phone book, I couldn't go anywhere without looking to see if there was a magic shop. When we visited my cousins in Sacramento, I would find and visit the local magic shop (called Misdirections) or when went to my grandma's in Oregon I found the Magic Man Novelty Shop. I can still feel the adrenaline and smell the Yellow Pages as I would barrel through the book to get to the M section. I have never since felt such exhilaration and anticipation as I did whenever I opened the phone book.

My favorite local shops were the Magic Shop in La Puente, K&L Magic in Claremont, Best Magic in the city of Anaheim, and the famous Hollywood Magic in Hollywood. My parents never complained about driving me all over Southern California to visit these places or about how long I would spend asking to see a demonstration of every trick in the store. For this I am forever grateful. There is nothing quite like the feel of a magic shop and I think it has to do with shared passion. Nobody owns a brick and mortar magic shop because it is a lucrative business. They do it because they love the art and because of that you can hang around all day just to talk with other people who are as passionate about the subject as you are. It is like a comic book store but you never feel less than because the guy behind the counter knows everything about Superman and you don't. It's just the greatest hang ever.

It is wild to me that for the longest time I never visited one of the most famous magic shops in the world and it was right down the street from my house in Azusa. Owen Magic Supreme has been making elite props for the world's greatest magicians since 1903. When I was a kid it was owned by Les and Gertrude Smith, who had been running it since 1963. I had driven by it many times and seen the iconic genie atop the building and the sign on the door that said *By Appointment Only*. And like Willy Wonka's Chocolate Factory, I could only imagine what incredible wonders lay inside.

One Saturday morning when I was about eleven, my dad said, "Let's go cruising." This activity was his version of the phone book search, the only difference being that he is still cruising and phone books are a thing of the past. We made our usual stop at the little Pepsi in a bottle store and then we turned down the street where Owen Magic was. My dad knew how much I loved to look at the outside of this building, so it was a regular part of our route, but this time we pulled into the driveway and parked. I looked at my dad in shock, thinking, *We don't have clearance for this, we are merely civilians.*

It turns out my dad had made a call to Les Smith and arranged some time for me to visit. He might as well have given me the Golden Ticket! That day I met Les, Gertrude, and their son, Alan, who continues to run the place today. They gave me a tour, showed me how Les turned magic wands and multiplying billiard balls on his lathe, and then we sat in the office and talked about magic for an hour and a half. As we left, while my feet hovered above the floor, Les put his arm around my shoulder and said, "Keep practicing, kid, and the next time you come back, bring some money." It was one of the best days ever.

Extra

I THINK OFTEN about what Les did for me that day. I had no money, no big Vegas show like his other clients, but he took the time to be present with me. What is funny to me is that he probably had no idea how big a deal that moment would still be for me today. This was ordinary for him. You see, one man's ordinary can every so often be another man's extraordinary. Every day he went to this place and made these things, but he sat with me as I experienced it for the first time. A couple hours of interrupting his schedule had such an impact on me. If you want to make a big impact, it comes through small actions. Take the time in the midst of business to see how you can be present with someone. I never again spent time with that man, but I have an appreciation for him that doesn't fade, because he took the time to care about me.

Moon Shoes

THERE USED TO be a toy store in every mall called K•B Toys. It was the number-one reason I got excited when my mom said we were heading to the mall to shop. One fall morning I was especially excited because I had saved twenty-nine dollars and was going to finally buy Moon Shoes. These futuristic-looking portable trampolines would strap onto your shoes and allow you to soar high in the air. The commercial claimed that you could jump like a kangaroo and reach to the moon. On top of how cool that sounded, having always been the kid who wore husky jeans, the idea of feeling weightless was especially intriguing.

We went to K•B Toys and picked them up. One size fits all, but they came in different colors. I should have noticed something fishy about the fact that a five-year-old and twelve-year-old could supposedly wear the same shoes, but I just assumed they worked because of science. It turns out that the science employed in Moon Shoes was a series of large rubber bands that stretched from the foot platform to a large plastic sleeve that went around the perimeter. I chose the green and purple color pattern, bought them with my own money, and couldn't wait to get home and try them out.

On the drive home I imagined how cool I would look doing my midair poses and how this must have been what Neil Armstrong felt like, knowing he was about to walk on the lunar surface (allegedly). We arrived home and I bolted from the car, through the front door, and scrambled up the stairs with the yellow K•B Toys bag in tow. I read the instructions, which essentially said "Jump," followed by a warning about the danger of embarking on such suicidal adventures. I climbed up to the top bunk of my bed, thinking that the higher I started the more air I would get when the "gravity bands" recoiled. I left the bed and everything went into slow motion, I could hear the cheers of my friends and the jealousy of strangers at school when they found out I had Moon Shoes.

Then . . . nothing happened. I landed and the rubber bands expanded under my weight and never returned to their original tautness. I jumped and again bottomed out on the carpet below. I had been tricked by "the man". My hard-earned dollars were spent—and I was left with a handful of magic beans and empty promises.

Extra

WE SAT QUIETLY for most of the car ride back to the mall. My mom could tell how disappointed I was, but she was always an encourager. Sometimes things aren't always as they seem, she explained; in an effort to make money, sometimes people can play on our emotions. Mom said just because they had a slick commercial and hired some "cool kid" from central casting, didn't mean the product itself was any good.

We have all had moments of being "had" like this. It can be disheartening. It is perhaps the opposite of the experience wonder gives us. While wonder gives us gifts and adds value, being had only seeks to take. It cements our feet to the ground. Our wings are clipped.

Looking back at this moment, though, I am grateful for the experience because it taught me some lessons that have helped me as someone who now runs his own business. The first being that we have a responsibility to bring a sense of goodwill to those we do business with. Integrity in marketing is more than just litigation avoidance, it is a reminder to put people ahead of profits and to serve people honestly. The second—and probably the most important thing I learned that day—is that one size never fits all.

Life Before Memory Cards

IT WAS JUST weeks before my sixth birthday and my parents had given me a choice: I could either get our old Atari video game console repaired or get a brand new 8-bit Nintendo Entertainment System. Before they could finish laying out their offer, I blurted out, "Nintendo!" Any kid growing up at this point in the '80s would have said the same thing. We had been watching the commercials nonstop—and I had even heard rumors that Lisa from my first-grade class had one at her house!

Nintendo had been out for a few years but this version had a combo pack including the Duck Hunt gun as well as R.O.B.—an actually robot that you could play the game with. Even though I been part of the decision, I was so filled with joy waiting for the big day and could not wait to open my presents.

The night of my birthday we met with family and friends at my favorite restaurant, Sir Pizza 'n' Stuff. This was a mom-and-pop version of a Shakey's Pizza, and it put the chain restaurant to shame. We played games, followed by a feast of pizza, chicken, and fried potato wedges that we all referred to as spuds. All that was left to do was open the presents.

The family watched as I opened each gift. My eyes

would regularly look over to the big box in the corner, knowing it was the ultimate gift. My parents did not let me down. Not only did I receive the NES Mega package, but I received what would be the most coveted game in all of kid-dom: The Legend of Zelda. Unlike its peers whose plastic covers were the kind of gray you only see in airport lobbies, Zelda's cartridge was made of solid gold. OK, it was painted gold, but it was shiny and I loved it!

This video game would become my obsession for the next several months. One thing you have to keep in mind about this time period is it was long before memory cards allowed you to save your game. Today most video games will save your progress and allow you to just continue playing where you left off last session. Back in my day (I have always wanted to say that), the only way to save your progress was to not die. You couldn't even shut the game off or you would be back to square one. We would just hit pause for essential breaks like snack time, running to the bathroom, or going to school.

After several months of attempting to save Zelda and win the game I decided I would devote an entire weekend to the conquest. This required me getting approval from the entire family as we only had one TV and I would be needing exclusive use. Somehow they said yes and it was on. I started Friday after school and apart from a small break for dinner, I played until late in the evening. I then paused the game, turned off just the TV and resumed the next morning. I repeated this process Saturday night and by Sunday morning I was nearly to the end of my quest. At this point my mom insisted I get a bath because my cousins were coming over for lunch and my dedication to this adventure had had quite a negative impact on my personal hygiene regime. I paused the game and ran to get clean. About fifteen minutes later I was dressed, refreshed, and ready to brag to my cousins about all I had accomplished. Then disaster struck.

I came into the living room to find that my cousin had started playing the game while I was gone—and because she didn't know what to do, she hit the reset button. All of my progress was erased. I was devastated. All of that work for nothing. Back to the beginning. I felt so discouraged. My cousin felt bad. Not bad enough, but she did apologize. To this day I have never reached the end of the game and helped liberate Zelda—because I was so bummed out about my work being lost that I stopped trying.

I am writing this story at an interesting moment, because in a way it feels like the year 2020 has pushed the reset button on my career. I know most entertainers feel that way. All that we worked for, the shows we booked, have all gone away in the midst of this global pandemic. I have no idea if and when people will gather in a theater again or feel comfortable choosing a playing card. However, reexamining this story from my youth is helping me find hope for today.

Extra

THE TRUTH IS when you end up having the reset button pushed in an area of your life, you aren't starting over at the beginning. You are a different person today, you have the skills and abilities that you developed by getting there the first time. Which means you are in a better position to build. Be encouraged knowing you will be able to get there quicker this time and make it better than it ever could have been before. This doesn't mean you shouldn't mourn the moment you are in. It's OK to be mad, but shift your frustration into action.

I wonder what would have happened if I had taken that route instead of never playing Zelda again. I let my frustration about what had happened keep me from moving forward and accomplishing the goal I had set out to accomplish. Part of why I am writing this book is because I don't want to get stuck in this moment of frustration. Sure, right now I am experiencing the effects of the reset button getting hit, but the question I need to ask is, "Where do I want to go from here?" I could be angry about what happened or I can view things through the eyes of wonder and ask, "What will I make happen *next*?"

Hot Coals

AFTER MY PARENTS' divorce, my mom was the first to remarry. My stepdad, Frank, had three daughters from a previous marriage, which meant that the kid dynamic in our home went from my sister and I to four girls and me. Later my dad would marry my stepmom, who also had three daughters, bringing the total to seven girls and one boy. I was caught in an outnumbered Brady Bunch scenario. Let's just say I played my fair share of dress-up and was in more than one Wham! cover band.

When you are a kid, moms tend to adopt certain rules to make a big deal about. Sure, they all agree on the basics, but each mom chooses a specialty to make the focus on nearly every conversation. Don't leave the cap off the toothpaste, if you make that face it will stay that way, and elbows off the table are some crowd favorites. However, for my mom the most important thing in the world for a season was, "Don't go outside without your shoes on."

Well, one day my sisters and I were especially bored. My oldest stepsister, Cyndi, is the one who came up with the brilliant idea: "Let's play follow the leader." To this day I am not sure why this game has the adolescent appeal that it does, but we couldn't have been more excited. We all hopped up out of our seats and began to mimic Cyndi's actions, which included bad John Travolta dance moves as we paraded around the living room.

Maybe it is the fact that as a kid you don't generally get to be in charge of others that makes us want to see how far people will go when playing this game. After a series of awkward dance moves and pathetic beatbox sounds, Cyndi decided to take it up a notch. She wanted to see if we would really follow her every move ... so she walked out the front door. I can still feel the exhilaration I felt walking outside on a Saturday afternoon without my shoes on. I imagined it was the same rush Marty McFly felt when he first hit eighty-eight miles per hour.

One by one we filed outside barefoot, down the driveway, and to the corner of our block. Our fearless leader hesitated for a second. Perhaps she was debating the trouble she might get into or maybe she was sizing us up to see if her troops had what it took. A second later she stepped into the crosswalk and one by one we unwaveringly followed her to the park across the street.

The park was busy that day but none of us cared what the strangers surrounding us thought of our ridiculous dance moves. We laughed and sang and had a ball. We were completely oblivious to the world around us and had no idea we were heading directly toward big trouble. The park had two large built-in barbecue grills. These were the old charcoal type that had a lever to allow you to dump out the old ash and make room for new coals the next time you wanted to cook.

That day someone had finished barbecuing and—rather than allow the coals to cool down in the grill—they dumped them out on the sidewalk in front of the playground. This must have happened just moments before we arrived, because as Cyndi's foot hit the first coals she let out a huge scream and started doing high knees like a football player at practice. We just figured this was another goofy dance move and one by one we screamed and without ever seeing the coals we copied her rather strange choreography, move for move, as we followed her, involuntarily performing an impromptu fire walk that would have impressed Tony Robbins himself!

Once we realized what had happened, panic set in and blisters popped out. We all huddled around the drinking fountain taking turns cooling our scorched feet from the ordeal. No matter how bad the pain got, we all were worried that it would pale in comparison to the lecture we would get from Mom. We waited for a while and then began the painful walk back home in order to receive what to this day is the world record for the longest "I told you so."

That was the first time I remember thinking that you should be very careful who you follow. That you can't assume the leader knows best just because they ended up with the title or that they see everything and are looking out for you. This is true in organizations and nations. Throughout history, blind faith has led to heartache and destruction. People stop wondering for themselves and just look to others to tell them how to act and think.

Several years ago I found myself near the top of an

org chart in a very unhealthy organization. Leadership was lacking in both heart and direction. What started as an initiative built on love and community had devolved into a production whose only objective was money and popularity. It didn't happen overnight, much like our game of follow the leader. Leadership slowly started making risky moves in the wrong direction and one by one the staff, volunteers, and community followed.

Extra

WHEN YOU'RE A kid and something that started out as a fun game becomes dangerous, it isn't very easy to stand up and say no. It may not be what you signed up for, but you still want to be a part of the group, you still want to play the game. I did the same thing for many years in this corporate environment. I justified my actions because I had to make a living and support my family. However, I also did things I am ashamed of and hurt people I loved because I wanted to be a part of something bigger than myself.

Then one day I started having some wonder-filled conversations with my wife. I wonder if we could find real community? I wonder if we could be in a healthier place as a family? I wonder if our careers and our passions could line up? These conversations helped us truly discover what decisions we had to make. I wouldn't trade the life we have now for anything, and it all changed because we allowed ourselves to wonder if there could be something extra in our ordinary.

Peeking at the Presents

I LOVE SURPRISES. The best part of Christmas morning for me when I was younger was not knowing what would be under the tree. A wrapped present is the embodiment of wonder. The possibilities are endless. This is probably why I love the art of magic. It is based entirely in the world of not knowing. However, when it comes to everyday life I sometimes find myself wanting to know exactly what I can expect and exactly what each day will hold. This approach will always set us up for disappointment because every day is full of the very real possibility of new surprises.

I remember the first time I realized that some surprises aren't great. Like dental surprises. As a child I had a huge fear of dentists. This is bad for a kid who had extra teeth and needed to have eleven adult teeth pulled.

One day I woke up and my mom had set clothes out for me that consisted of a pair of shorts and a T-shirt. The school I attended had a pretty strict dress code: I had to wear dress pants and collared shirts. So I was elated, thinking she was keeping me out of school to go to Disneyland. The truth was she was taking me to have a major dental surgery. Surprise!

Not long after that my dad took me for a bike ride.

We were riding on the sidewalk near a local shopping center having a great time when a car came out of the parking lot and knocked me into the street. I wasn't hurt, just very surprised. I was more shocked when—after my dad and the stranger made sure I was OK—I got hit by a car a second time five minutes later. Now that was surprising!

In high school when Katie and I started dating she woke up one day to the surprise that her dog had gotten into a fight with a skunk and then rolled around on everything in her room. She frantically cleaned up and got ready for school only to find out upon arrival that we could all smell the skunk on her backpack. She threw it away and carried her books the rest of the day.

Probably the most surprised I have ever been was when my mom called a family meeting before church one Sunday. She had been dating my now stepdad for a while and all his kids were at the house that morning as she happily told us that later that day at the family BBQ they were going to get married. All our relatives coming over had no idea they were going to be part of a surprise wedding. (Although everyone at youth group did know because my sister Sara can't keep a secret to save her life.)

Surprises can be wonderful or painful—and often the temptation is to think that if we just knew what was going to happen we would be happier. I learned this wasn't the case one Christmas when I thought I would sneak a peek at my presents. It did not end well.

I was six years old and I had known what I wanted for Christmas since July. The He-Man action figure and cartoon star was pretty huge in my world. I had been lucky enough to receive the Castle Grayskull play set which He-Man was currently living in, but he was desperately in need of some transportation. Imagine how embarrassing it must have been for him to be the Master of the Universe and still have to take public transportation. Luckily a new TV commercial let me know that I was in need of a giant robotic spider that he could ride.

One Friday in early December I went to spend the weekend with my dad. Early the next morning I went to brush my teeth and noticed something wedged between the cabinet and the wall. I reached my little hand back and found a brand-new Nintendo video game called Spelunker. For a second I thought it was strange because my dad didn't have a Nintendo . . . and then I realized it must be one of my Christmas presents!

What a happy accident! I had wanted this game for a while and now I knew I was gonna get it! Then I began to wonder what *other* treasures my dad might be hiding. He was asleep in the living room still. (For as long as I can remember my dad has watched TV till all hours of the night and then fallen asleep in his recliner. Although he has a bed, I don't think he has ever used it. You may think it would be uncomfortable to sleep in a chair all night but my father once fell asleep standing up at a funeral.)

So with Dad asleep in the other room, I decided to do what I had seen in so many movies—snoop for my presents. I checked all the classic spots. In the closet, behind the door . . . eventually I checked under the bed and to this day I swear the light from the window shone on the treasure like a scene from Indiana Jones. There, before my eyes was a bright gold K•B Toys bag. I reached under the bed and pulled back the top of the bag to reveal the He-Man Spider vehicle!

I was so excited for about twenty seconds. And then I realized that for the next three weeks I had to act like I didn't know what I was getting. I became the most paranoid kid on the planet. For the rest of time leading up to Christmas all the excitement and joy was gone. I was just left with an uncomfortable feeling knowing I would have to act surprised when I opened it. I even rehearsed my reactions in the mirror. It was awful.

Extra

IT IS ROMANTIC to think that if we just knew what was going to happen we would all handle it responsibly. I have found that for myself uncertainty of the future is not a curse, it is a blessing. Every day you wake up not knowing what will happen and yet endless possibilities are available to you. Freedom comes when we learn to embrace wonder for the gift that it is. Remember, no matter how challenging life may feel, a wonderful surprise may just be right around the corner. Just be sure if you do go around the corner to get it, you look for cars!

Be Undeniably Good

MY ENTRY INTO professional showbiz was performing for birthday parties in my early teenage years. It was strange for many reasons—the first being I was often the same age or just a few years older than the kids I was there to entertain. There were many times I would show up to the party, greet the parents, and immediately see the shock on their faces that they had hired a "kid" to perform at their event. The only thing better than seeing this expression was seeing the satisfied look on their face after the show, when they'd seen their guests actually had a great time. Meanwhile, I couldn't believe I was getting paid to do the one thing I would do for free anytime someone asked.

Now before you get too excited, these venues were not the most glamorous locations for an up-and-coming star to make his appearance. The set up was almost always the same: a backyard party with some rented chairs, a tent for shade, and a bounce house. I hate bounce houses! There is nothing more distracting to a group of kids than a bounce house. Let's face it: they are fun, really fun. Unless you are the young magician that has been hired to perform a show for the kids. I remember one show during which I did a routine that required me to be blindfolded—and when I removed the blindfold, every child had left my show to go into the bounce house. It was that day that I added into my contract, *All bounce houses must be unplugged for the duration of the performance.*

Extra

THESE SHOWS WERE exhausting, often performed in full sunlight without shade and very rarely did the effects get the reaction I assumed they deserved. However, they taught me countless life lessons and skills that I use every day as a full-time professional. One of these things is a lesson I later heard Steve Martin coin perfectly: "Be undeniably good." It is one thing to entertain people who bought a ticket and showed up at the theater. It is another to be able to capture the attention of a group of rib-eating family and friends who don't need an icebreaker to get things started. If you can kill in a backyard for people who were surprised with a show, you will have no problem surviving in the entertainment business.

It was also during these shows I realized that entitlement is not your friend. Standing in front of people with a microphone doesn't make you a leader. Sheer volume doesn't equal influence. You earn the right to be heard when you show people that you care and that you are not just there for a paycheck. In my line of work the client who hires you can tell this by how you carry yourself, the way you welcome an audience, your choice of material, and the choice to make it about others and not yourself. Whatever path you choose for your career, always put people ahead of profit, and you will have extraordinary results.

Stories Are Magic

IF YOU HAVEN'T noticed by this point, I love storytelling. It amazes me that most of us are so obsessed with other people's stories (i.e., the royal wedding, our Facebook friends' Hawaii vacation, the reality TV stars' backstory) that we never take the time to see what is so extraordinary about our own journey. It is time to embrace and appreciate the story of your life. To make the most of the stories that have made you. I have learned that most people are unknowingly awesome.

When we take things at face value, we can underestimate the significance of everyday life events—and yet when we talk to others and hear their stories, we are amazed at how incredible their lives seem. They are ordinary stories but with a little something extra. This book is first and foremost a product of self-examination. A way of forcing myself to come to terms with the experiences that shaped my life. In the process of reflecting on these moments, I realized that this practice could be incredibly beneficial for all of us, so I am inviting you to join me.

The tradition of telling stories has existed as long as language has been around. Ever since humans first huddled around a fire to keep warm, stories have been one of our primary ways of communication. There is something incredibly powerful about communicating through story. Even Jesus primarily chose parables and storytelling as a way of communication.

I remember being a kid going to a private school where they invited guest speakers into the chapel to give encouraging talks on character and how we could make a difference. I heard one presenter after another talk about the incredible challenges and adversity they faced. My immediate thought was always, *I haven't been through what they have so how could I do what they are doing?* But the best thing about your story is it is different from everyone else who has ever lived. The truth is, though, it isn't just enough to tell your story. Great storytellers not only know the uniqueness of their journey but see the principles and tools that can be universally applied to each of our individual paths.

The world needs to hear your unique story. I remember watching Phil Rosenthal, the creator of the hit TV show *Everybody Loves Raymond*, talking about what made that show so appealing to people. What I took away from his talk was the more he got into the personal specifics of how his family operated, the more people related to it. Making it specific didn't alienate people, it simply showed that we are all on the same planet experiencing similar challenges, desires, and frustrations. The better you understand your own life story and journey, the better you will understand your neighbor.

I performed magic for twenty-five years before I gave people a chance to know me on stage. Up until then, the show was full of surface level fun. I was worried that if I got too personal or vulnerable, people wouldn't get the escape they sometimes come to a show needing. Embracing storytelling has redefined my performances and brought along with it some interesting side effects.

First, people relate to it more. They leave connected with the show because they are reminded, challenged, or encouraged to take an action. Second, the audience leaves knowing me. I used to say I want people to leave thinking to themselves, *I would like to have a drink with that guy.* Now my goal is that they leave feeling like they just did.

Extra

GROWTH HAPPENS THROUGH relationships and relationships are developed through the sharing of stories. How many meetings have you had where you say, "Yeah, we didn't really connect, we just talked about the weather, sports, movies, and so on." Other times you leave thinking, *That was great! I told them about the time* ... [insert personal experience here]. Learning to share your story will have a huge impact on your personal relationships.

We have all met someone who thought they were a great storyteller but they were just long-winded. You've been cornered at a party by the guy who wouldn't stop talking about [insert boring topic here]. There are some keys I have uncovered to telling compelling stories, and I would like to share them so you can be more effective in communicating professionally and personally. Not just telling stories, but doing so in an extraordinary way.

Value and love your story. Even if it is a scary story. Some of us are afraid of our story. When you learn to share your story it puts you in the driver's seat. You become the narrator. Like the voice on every episode of the TV show *The Wonder Years*. The narrator doesn't just tell us what happened, he leads us down a path of discovery. You get to choose how to tell your story. What story do you want to tell? What do you want to leave people with? You get to choose how others experience your story.

The characters of a story always affect the arc. Who you allow in your life will shape the outcome of your story—so only let good people in. This happens in movies, right? A new character shows up and it all goes to hell. Never forget that you are the casting director of your story. Some of us act like we are junior high drama teachers and we are just making the most of the cast we are given. *You* are in charge of your story. If someone in your life is negatively impacting your arc, write them out of it.

When you share your story with others, you have the opportunity to build deep connections. I was recently in Orlando, Florida, for a series of shows and I posted on Instagram that I was coming to town. A friend I have known for a couple of years instantly left a comment saying, "I am in town as well!" We texted each other and made plans to meet up. That evening was a blast. We laughed, explored the city, and ate way too much food. A few hours into our hang time he mentioned how crazy it was that we had only seen each other in person once before.

I was shocked. No way this could be true, because it seriously felt like we had known each other since we were kids. The truth is we'd met two years before at an event we both just happened to be working. After the program we decided to hang out with the crew rather than just heading our separate ways. This became our custom after each of the three nights we were working this event, and it had a summer camp vibe. Each person those nights shared stories from their lives, and we all left that event as friends.

If you want to practice sharing a story from your life, pick a moment in time that was a turning point for you. Perhaps it was when someone entered or exited your life, a new job, or a move to a new town. Write down what your life or mindset was like prior to that moment. Then write down the experience of the moment itself. Follow that with a thought about how your life or mindset changed after that experience. Then share that story with a friend. I guarantee that by taking the time to recognize, write down, and share your story, not only will your friend get to know you better, you will also get to know yourself in a new way.

Extra Ordinary Places

WHEN I WAS a kid my grandparents lived in Long Beach, California, which was about an hour from our house. We used to go visit them on the weekends and would take trips to Shoreline Village. Each trip included a ride or two on the carousel and, of course, a stop at the magic shop. My grandfather had just recently retired from McDonnell Douglas, where he built airplanes for a living. I would often brag about him on the playground when a plane would fly over. I would say to my buddies, "Yeah, he probably made that wing." He even brought me home some NASA stickers from a recent mission he had helped with. Needless to say, he was the coolest.

My grandma had worked at the Pacific Bell phone company as a switchboard operator, way back when you had to tie the lines in by hand. They had both worked very hard and wanted to retire somewhere peaceful. They chose a little piece of heaven in southern Oregon called Grants Pass. As a kid I had no idea how big California was. We never traveled too far, so when my mom told me that we were going to see my grandparents new house one state up and that we would be in the car for twelve hours, I couldn't believe it. We eventually would make this trip twice a year and I got used to it, but that first journey was quite epic!

We loaded up in the family car, a Ford Tempo, which was not known for its legroom. My sister Sara has always been tall and we made an arrangement that she would lie on the seat and I got to have the whole floor. You heard me right, I did a twelve-hour drive lying on the floor with no seat belt! This is before the Click It or Ticket seat belt law was in effect. I do wonder why my parents didn't see the value in them prior to this, but that is a personal conversation I should have.

Previously my grandparents' house was small and packed in by other houses on either side, so when we turned off the country road onto their private driveway that seemed to go *forever*, I couldn't believe it. They had a massive front yard and a creek that ran through it. In the back was a garden with rows of apple trees and my grandpa had his own workshop. This place was magic to me.

We walked in the door and my grandmother told us she had gone grocery shopping to buy our favorite things, and she even had a fresh glass of strawberry Quik sitting on the table just for me. If you have not had strawberry Quik, put a bookmark here and immediately go acquire some. When I was a kid I couldn't fathom that grown-ups could have this delicious pink nectar anytime they wanted to. Grandma continued to have strawberry Quik for me as a tradition even when I was a grown man and brought my kiddos to visit.

Grants Pass is by all accounts an ordinary place, but for me it had all the extra I needed. For those who call it home it is just a normal city, but for my family it became an oasis. Twice a year we would take this trek and each time we would add new items to the list of must-do things while we were in town. I would visit the two local magic shops, we would drive to Medford and tour the Harry and David factory that served all sorts of treats. We would go park hopping, visit the giant caveman statue, and play in the creek. We even rode the jet boats that raced down the river and then stopped, immediately soaking everyone on board.

My favorite things to do, though, were to just tag along with my grandparents while they did their favorite activities. For my grandpa it was either hanging out in his shed or going to breakfast with a group of friends my grandmother called his old cronies. In the shed my grandpa would take me through his toolbox and show me all the items he used at his job. After he passed, my grandmother gave me his bright orange tool box covered in aerospace stickers. It is one of my prized possessions.

He would even let me drive his "tractor"—a small, red, ride-on lawnmower that he used to mow his incredible yard. He took such pride in that piece of land! I can still hear the sound of the sprinkler he would move around the yard as we sat on the large covered porch and just enjoyed the fresh air. Grandpa loved being at home so much that the only time I ever remember him leaving was when he would go to meet the cronies for breakfast. This gathering happened at one of two places—it was either Burger King or a little diner that served toast with sausage gravy on it. Grandpa would laugh every time he told me that in the army they called it shit on a shingle.

Gramps and his crew were quite the cast of characters. My Uncle Homer was Grandpa's brother and always wore inappropriate baseball hats. Each one had a different dirty phrase that I would later realize the meaning of and blush with embarrassment. They would all take turns sharing stories and my grandfather would always sing his favorite Irish drinking song that was about a little mouse who got into the whiskey and demanded to fight the cat. Grandpa would sing this tune at the top of his lungs and every rendition ended with him laughing so hard he would cry. The last few tears always felt different as his smile melted away and you could tell he was remembering times that were special.

Grandpa had gained quite a bit of weight since his army days, so much that the tattoo on his forearm was nothing more than a stretched-out ink blob. I would tease him and ask what the tattoo was supposed to be and he would say, "Can't you see anything? That's an American flag with an eagle on it." This wasn't the worst tattoo in our family, though. My dad's dad had a gotten so drunk the night before he entered the service that he woke up with a tattoo of his social security number on one arm and the name of a woman he has no memory of on the other.

I would laugh at the inappropriate jokes Grandpa's friends told (though they flew over my head) and then we would ride back to the house in his little pickup truck that smelled of pipe tobacco and only had one Willie Nelson 8-track tape. To this day I can't listen to Willie

Nelson without thinking of Grandpa and crying. I also cry when I hear Neil Diamond, but that's just because his voice is so painful to listen to.

My grandmother also had her rituals. She was the social butterfly and would often be at a church function or making runs for her Jafra Cosmetics business. Say what you will about multilevel marketing schemes, but my grandmother's complexion was impeccable. Every morning she would wake up before sunrise, make a cup of coffee, sit in a chair reading her Bible, and start a new sewing project she had no intention of finishing. On particularly cold mornings when it was too chilly to sleep in, I would build a fire for her in the fireplace and sit down on the floor by her with a deck of cards. She would read the Bible while I practiced how to cheat at cards—it couldn't have been more perfect.

Extra

THERE WASN'T ONE specific thing that made this place spectacular. It was simply extra ordinary in every way. I have since met people who are from Grants Pass and they laugh when I talk about it so nostalgically. Similarly to how people from all over the world come to where we live in Southern California for vacation. Somehow, though, my grandparents made it special for us—their only agenda being how they could make every moment of our trip wonderful. So much so that even now that they have both passed, I have a deep connection to this place.

We all have our own getaways. A place that when we are there breaks us out of our current reality. The more I grow older, I realize that these places are not as important as the mindset we have while we are in them. Think of a place you love and describe why you love it. I always end up saying things like *it is peaceful* or *I can just rest when I am there*. The truth is if you woke up at home and then took a flight to Hawaii, the difference is not just geographical. More than a change of scenery, you have had a change of mindset.

Now imagine the possibilities if—without leaving your desk at work—you could have your mind shifted to that place of peace. We all have this ability; whether your practice is meditation or prayer, you can allow yourself a moment to breathe and reflect. Too often we are just living for those two weeks out of the year when we can get away from it all. Wouldn't it be more powerful if instead of escaping our ordinary we could bring the extra to it, so it became special for everyone else? What a privilege it is for us to be able to bring that mindset of hope, rest, and peace everywhere we go. The next time you are struggling to shake off negativity or feeling like you just need to be somewhere different, think instead about how you *can* be someone different in the situation you are in. It just takes a minor shift to see the wonder that is all around you. After all, Strawberry Quik, if you think about it, is just extra ordinary milk.

Blackstone's Warehouse

THERE WASN'T A more iconic name in magic when I was a kid than Harry Blackstone Jr. It was his face plastered across the front of the magic kit my parents bought me when I was seven years old. His father was a magician before him and a peer of Houdini. They were the last great dynasty of magicians in America. I saw him perform on TV countless times; he was everything you wanted a magician to be. He levitated assistants, produced rabbits he would then give away to kids in the audience, and even had custom bedazzled tuxedos that glittered like a mirror ball all the way to the back of the auditorium. Not to mention his unforgettable baritone voice, the kind of voice that you would swear filled a theater without the need for microphones.

When we were twelve, my buddy Cody surprised me by getting tickets for us to see Blackstone's touring show. It was a huge spectacular. A cast of forty, costumes and sets like I'd never seen. He performed his famous floating light bulb and when it flew out from the stage and over my head in the twelfth row, I said quiet audibly, "I give up!" I have always had this ability to shut off the analytical side of my brain when watching a magic show. The truth is I know how most magic works but I can still enjoy it like a five-year-old kid. I consider this a superpower that only serves me, and I love it.

Blackstone's full evening show was the ultimate magical experience and included a meet and greet in the lobby directly after the performance. We quickly joined the others in line to buy our posters and get our programs signed by the master magician. As we waited in the queue, I took the time to rehearse in my head exactly what I would say to the great Blackstone. I would tell him in detail how my parents bought me his magic set when I was a mere seven years old, and how it started me on my show business path, and how I recently started performing for local birthday parties, for pay, and pizza slices, and how it was all thanks to him. However, when we got to the front of the line, all of my grand thoughts of becoming fast friends with Mr. Blackstone were quickly reduced to me just staring at him, with a rather insipid smile plastered on my face.

For years I regretted that moment of being completely tongue-tied and awestruck, feeling like I missed an opportunity to connect with one of my heroes. Harry passed a few years later, and I thought again about how I wish we had connected more. One day I was sitting at home when the phone rang. It was a lady with a very welcoming voice and she said, "Is this Taylor?" I said, "Yes." She asked if I was a magician and I replied yes, then she asked if I live in Azusa and I thought, *This is getting creepy*. She told me her name was Mrs. Blackstone, that she was Harry's widow and former stage partner as well. Then she told me something that blew my mind.

I did not know that for many years the Blackstone family had kept their secret warehouse of illusions in my home town! Azusa, California! It was just a few blocks from my house and I never knew it. In fact, it was the unmarked building next door to Owen Magic Supreme. Mrs. Blackstone went on to tell me that since Harry's passing they had been renting his props for TV shows and movie productions. She had been looking for some young magicians in the area who could help around the warehouse.

I took her up on the offer, and as soon as I arrived at the warehouse, my mind was blown—nearly a century's worth of magic props, costumes, and set pieces were packed and stacked in this massive space! All of a sudden I was surrounded by props that previously I had only read about in books or seen on TV—and they had been here in my neighborhood the whole time. It was there in that warehouse of wonder, surrounded by reminders of his life and legacy, that I felt like I finally connected to one of my childhood heroes, even after he'd passed. It is an experience I am so grateful to have had.

Extra

MY TIME HELPING at the Blackstone warehouse taught me many things, but perhaps the most important is that you *never know* when your next wonderful adventure might take place. It could be right around the corner or right under your nose. Many times we think we have to go somewhere far away to experience amazement, but wonder is around you everywhere, in your own community. Never underestimate the possibilities that surround you every day. Every phone call has the potential to change your life, every conversation with a neighbor is an opportunity to impact others for good. You just have to be willing to say yes to the opportunities when they come.

One fun story from the Blackstone warehouse is that all of the cases were painted bright orange. This served a very practical purpose because the Blackstone family for decades had traveled in with large semitrucks full of equipment and would often have to train a local crew upon arrival. Loading out was easy because the only instructions you needed was that anything orange goes back on the truck. Rumor has it that Blackstone senior often traveled with a can of orange paint and if he happened to really like a set piece at a local theater it would mysteriously be painted orange by the end of the run. I am not condoning theft, but it is an interesting thought when we talk about seizing opportunities.

Too many people wait to make a move out of fear, but in life you have to take action. If you want to create something, make it. I am not suggesting that anyone is self-made—we are all products of our environments and the people we choose to surround ourselves with— however, no one else is the supervisor of your life. Don't wait for permission; chances are no one else is thinking about how they can fulfill your dreams. At the end of the day it's on you to make the move. In other words, if opportunity strikes, paint it orange.

The Art of Navigation

I REMEMBER BEING a kid and daydreaming about the incredible jobs I might one day have. I always loved entertainment and music, so I was pretty certain I would either become a magician or the lead guitarist in a famous rock band. These were the only two options in my futile brain. OK, there was a third . . . but who is going to hire a lead guitarist who performs magic? So imagine my surprise when my mother arranged for me to start a job the summer of my fifteenth birthday that had nothing to do with my dreams of performing. What I had thought was just a meal with some of her friends from church turned out to be a job interview that felt more like an arranged marriage.

The Wilsons were longtime friends of my parents who also happened to own an appliance store. We talked over dinner about how they needed help around their shop since business had picked up, and then Mr. Wilson asked what I did for work. I mentioned that other than magic shows I wasn't working yet. I had just gotten a work permit and would begin the job hunt soon. Since I had my mind set on working at a music store or magic shop, I didn't realize what was happening right in front of me. The next thing I knew, I would start at the appliance store first thing the next morning.

I was still in shock when the alarm went off at 6:00 a.m. two weeks into summer break. The whole thing felt unnatural. I sat on the front porch waiting for Bob, another employee who would be picking me up and taking me to the shop. Sure enough, at 6:25, still half asleep, I climbed into a stranger's van to head to a job I did not want to do.

When we arrived at the store about ten minutes later, things started to look up. I got a tour from Mr. Wilson, who showed me through his store, which had not only appliances but also big-screen TVs, surround-sound CD players, and VCRs. I started to imagine myself becoming salesman of the month and furnishing my bachelor pad with all these amazing items that I was able to buy with my huge bonus and employee discounts. My daydream ended about the same time Mr. Wilson said, "Time to load the truck.

It turns out that my role did not require me to be the Don Draper of appliances. Instead I would be cleaning the store bathroom, loading large appliances on the truck, and then joining Bob on his delivery/setup calls. We loaded a fridge, a big-screen TV, and a home entertainment system into the store box truck and started on our way. It took about two minutes of real conversation for me to realize that Bob was quite a quirky fellow.

Bob grew up in Minnesota and loved Pepsi, which he called pop. I always just called it Pepsi or soda. Pop, to me, was a name for Dad. Which is why it was weird when he asked me if I liked pop. . . . Like him? I love him. By the time we departed the store at 8:00 a.m., he was already finishing his second can of the day, and he literally wanted every last drop. As he drove the gigantic truck with one hand, his other would tilt the can upside down as he used his first two fingers in a drumlike fashion to try and force the few remaining drops from the bottom of the can. This procedure was much louder than you would imagine and went on while we passed several exits on the freeway.

Bob did most of the talking—about his childhood in Minnesota, his dream of raising sled dogs, and of course his love for pop. He had a million stories and it seemed like he had lived a pretty full life, though looking back, now, he was probably in his early thirties at the time. I asked Bob where we were heading and he told me the address of the client. When I followed up with, "Where is that?" he simply responded by tossing me a Thomas Guide map book and said, "You tell me, you're the navigator!"

You see, this was the mid-nineties and although the Internet was around, we hadn't yet decided it would run every decision we made. There were no smartphones or GPS devices at this time. Just a large collection of spiral-bound maps with grids you needed to learn how to read and understand . . . and navigate. You would start with the address of where you wanted to end up, figure out where you were currently, and then navigate the road in between to get to your destination. There were no apps that told you the fastest route or when to leave in order to beat traffic. Sometimes you would realize that the route you set out on was not going to work and you would have to make a new plan.

It was a long summer and a crash course into the job force. However, I was able to buy a new guitar with my earnings and when school started . . . I never went back to the shop again.

Extra

I LEARNED SO much that summer working for the Wilsons and driving with Bob. I learned that you can get along with just about anyone if you choose to see the value in their story. I learned so many handy tips—like how to remove the doors from a fridge that is too big to fit through a doorway, a trick I have employed twice in my married life. I also learned that I definitely did not want to make a career in the appliance business!

However, the biggest thing that I learned on my first job came from using that Thomas Guide. I think in life we are so scared that we might not end up where we want to be. In our relationships, in our careers. We can be so hesitant to make a move because what if it is the wrong decision or, worse, we let someone else tell us what to do because that is what worked for them.

So many people have let the fact that they don't know how to do what they want to do stop them from doing anything. That map book taught me something great: there is more than one way to get there. Sure, you might have to recalculate, the journey might take you longer based on the road conditions, but the sooner you get started the sooner you will get there. It starts with knowing where you want to end up, discovering where you are now, and then navigating the road in between. Many of us might be asking God or the universe, "How do we get there?" I think the honest response to that question would be, "You tell me, you're the navigator."

Just Keep the Kids Alive

AFTER I LEFT my job at the appliance store I started working as an elementary school day care counselor. I would work at a private elementary school before and after going to school myself. From 6:00 a.m. until 8:00 a.m. and again from 3:00 p.m. to 6:00 p.m. each day we would care for the kids whose parents worked full-time jobs. We would plan crafts, games, and activities. The truth is our job was basically to keep the kids alive until their parents picked them up.

At least that is how the job was explained to me by Josh, the senior counselor on duty. He and I were paired up to watch a class of twenty-five kindergartners. The kids and Josh were so fun that I knew I was going to enjoy working there. What I didn't know is working with people is sometimes messy. As Josh and I were watching over the playground on my first day, I noticed one of the kids had a sneaky look on his face. He was hanging out by one of the big trees on the playground and looking over his shoulder as if to see if anyone was paying attention. His back was turned to us and as I wondered what he was doing, I saw a stream of liquid passing from him to the tree . . . He was peeing!

I had been camping a lot as kid and had done my fair

share of using nature's toilet. As freeing as it may be, this is not something that should be done every day and certainly not out in the open on school grounds. I didn't know what to do, so I yelled, "Hey, you can't do that!" This is when I learned that you should let them finish first, because I startled the poor boy. Then he zipped up quickly and peed all over himself.

I looked at Josh, who immediately leapt into action. "We got a wet one," he said over the walkie-talkie, then requested a replacement so he could walk our young friend to the office to get cleaned up. Jessica, one of our coworkers, came over to support me with the class while Josh was gone. I was still in shock and completely unprepared for what happened next.

I looked over toward the monkey bars where several kids were climbing. I noticed one of the girls toward the top of the gym was taking a big step to the next bar when she paused and got a glazed look in her eyes. A second later the floodgates opened and she peed all over the jungle gym below. "You've got to be kidding me!" I cried out. About that time Josh came back from the office, and without skipping a beat, Jessica took the little girl to the office so she could get cleaned up.

Josh told me this was a regular occurrence, that these kiddos were adjusting to a new schedule, new people, and a new place. They didn't always think ahead, and as a result, accidents happened. We can't always prevent them, we just have to take care of them as they learn, he said. This very teachable moment was interrupted when we walked over to the jungle gym to block the area and found that some of the boys were using the now wet sand below to make mud pies. Have I mentioned that people are messy?

Extra

I WONDER WHAT would happen if we treated everyone with the same forgiveness and understanding we give to children. I wonder what would happen if we realized that we never know where people are coming from. They might be adjusting to a new situation and they might have some accidents along the way. Our job as fellow humans is not to judge or criticize people when they fail; instead, we are to help them up. Through compassion and acceptance, we can help them clean up the mess and point out the good we see in them.

One of my favorite memories on the playground was a few months later with a little boy named TJ. I was so intrigued by this five-year-old—and not because we shared the same initials but because he embodied wonder in everything he did. He had an avid imagination and was always creating his own adventures. One day Josh and I were making the rounds on the field when we saw TJ carrying his backpack toward the recently christened jungle gym. Even though it had been professionally cleaned since the incident, most kids avoided the structure so we watched, wondering what TJ had planned.

He unzipped his backpack and removed a plastic grocery bag from inside it. With the bag in his right hand he scaled to the very top of the structure and stood balanced on high. As we watched, he slowly put one arm in each handle of the bag and held his thumbs to his chest like a soldier ready for battle. At this point Josh and I looked at each other and yelled, "Parachute!" The entire world went into slow motion as we ran toward TJ as he began his free fall.

We reached the playground just seconds after he belly flopped into the sandbox. Just then I remembered Josh's simple job description, "Just keep the kids alive." TJ slowly lifted his face toward us, now caked with sand and drool. With that same attitude of wonder he asked us the question he was dying to know: "Did it puff up?"

That day TJ may have had an accident, he may have made a poor choice. While we eventually talked about the importance of safety with him and why TV shows always say *don't try this at home*, the first thing we did was let him know that it *did* puff up! We cleaned him up and took him to the school nurse, but made sure we didn't squash his desire for wonder. Maybe you have a friend, neighbor, or family member who in an effort to have an adventure made a poor choice. I wonder what would happen if—instead of pointing out their obvious mistakes—we helped them in the midst of their mess to explore what else might be out there for them?

A Tale of Two Teachers

WE CAN ALL point to teachers who have had a profound impact on our lives. My first-grade teacher Ms. B was magical. My parents and I had taken a tour of the school before deciding I would attend there. When I entered her class for the first time I saw something extra. I'd been in other, ordinary classrooms. While other teachers' classrooms had similar stock decorations and inspirational posters, everything in Ms. B's room was handmade and original. You could tell just by the way she set up the room that this job was a passion for her and not an obligation.

She was the kind of teacher that made you look forward to school. Learning became an adventure and creativity was valued more than perfection. Best of all, her brother worked for the Häagen-Dazs ice cream company and every Friday he would bring a selection of the most amazing frozen treats. Thirty-three years later I have yet to taste an ice cream as delicious as those fudge bars he brought every Friday.

When Ms. B spoke, she commanded the room with warmth and compassion. I can't remember a time she had to scold or reprimand a student for their behavior, although I am sure it happened. She just had this way of being that made you feel comfortable to try your best, knowing that if you made a mistake it would be OK and we would work through it together. She created an environment of inclusion and encouragement.

This is the first time I remember feeling what it was like to be on a team. I was proud to be in Ms. B's class. Whenever there was a schoolwide competition or challenge goal like the Book It! reading program or the magazine drive, we would try extra hard because we felt like we were doing it for Ms. B. She had our full attention and respect and never once had to demand it.

Then there was another teacher. You know the teacher I am talking about. The kind that would read books about Stalin and Mussolini (not for historical purposes but to get material). Every school had a teacher like this and when their name was mentioned, children would react like Hogwarts students hearing the name Voldemort. However, ours went by the name Mrs. P.

Mrs. P was my fifth-grade teacher and she was downright mean. She set the ground rules from day one: we were here to learn and not to have fun. This seemed ridiculous to me; after all, I had spent a year with Ms. B and knew how much fun could be had in the process of learning. The worst part about being assigned to my new fifth-grade class was that it was a combo class with sixth grade. That meant that she would be my teacher for two years in a row!

While her overall anxiety and frustration was visible whenever she addressed the class, it really kicked into gear when you were talking to her face-to-face. She had all of the classic teacher decorations that would make you think she was on your side, including a wooden sign on her desk that read *There is no such thing as a stupid question*. Once I walked up to her desk, really excited about my new erasable ink pen. I showed her the pen and asked if I could use it on my math homework. She replied, "That is a stupid question." I immediately held up her sign so she could see it. The rest of math class I spent waiting to see the principal.

Every kid hates the idea of seeing the principal. That's when you know you're in real trouble. If you see the principal it most definitely means your parents will get a call, which means double trouble. Not to mention the fact that I went to a private school where the parents and kids signed an agreement allowing the principal to swat you with a paddle . . . Yeah, that really happened. I never got swat but I did hear it happening once, and to this day if someone introduces themselves to me and says they are a school principal, my brain thinks, *We should keep an eye on this person*.

One time in Mrs. P's class, I was leaning on my left arm. She called on me and when I went to lift up my head, my arm came with it. I had recently gotten braces and my shirtsleeve got caught on them. The weirdness of the situation made the whole class bust up laughing. The teacher thought I did it on purpose and seeing that she had lost control of her class, she sent me to the principal.

I was terrified as I walked with my arm sewn to my tooth all the way to the principal's office. I entered the door with my forearm acting as a mask and began to explain the situation. I finished my muffled story and the entire office erupted with laughter. A few of the staff helped me get unstuck and offered me refuge and a Diet Coke in the teachers' lounge until lunchtime. Who knows what was going on in Mrs. P's life? I was too young to understand where she was coming from. The only thing I remember was how she made me feel.

Extra

EVEN THOUGH THEIR names may be different, we have all met these two teachers. Maybe for you they were two supervisors, two doctors, or two ministers. When we are given the opportunity to lead other people we are also given the responsibility to care for them. The question we must be able to answer is whether we will lead out of authority or love. Leading out of authority is the ordinary approach, but we are looking to bring something extra, aren't we?

Real leadership equates to influence, and all of us have influence over someone. It could be a younger sibling, a coworker, or even a neighbor. We want to lead in a way that shows we are working on behalf of others, that shows we see the bigger picture of what we as a group are trying to build. Don't be an ordinary leader, be someone who brings the extra.

On the surface there isn't much about these two teachers that points to one being more successful than the other. Both wanted to influence others, both hoped for respect and the ability to lead others. At the end of the day the major difference is found in what drove them to seek leadership. One was fueled by seeing the students succeed. The other wanted influence because of what it meant for her and not because of what she could do for others with that influence.

When you take the approach in leadership that my first-grade teacher took, not only will you gain respect and influence, but it will also be accompanied by joy. I have tried this both ways, in business and in my personal life. I noticed that whether leading a team at work or just trying to raise your children, people will know what is in your heart when they see how you lead. The times I have demanded to be heard because of my authority have never gone well. When we lean into loving others, things will fall into place.

The implications of our actions stretch far beyond our relationship with individuals. How you are at work defines what many people think about your business. Think right now about a company you dislike or a store you won't shop at. Now think about why you feel that way. Most likely it is because you had a negative experience with an employee, and it seems that must be how the whole place is run. How would your opinion differ if your encounter with that employee had been positive? What you do with the influence you have will have a ripple effect for years to come.

So what do you want others' experience to be of you, your family, and your business? The best part is we get to write the characters we play in other people's stories. When they talk about us, will it be like an ice cream party or like a trip to the principal's office? Let's make sure our actions line up with those intentions. If you want to have influence that makes a difference, you need to be different. You need to be extraordinary.

Elementary School Famous

IF YOU ASKED me who I wanted to be like when I was a kid, there was only one answer: the Weepul man. If you grew up in the 1980s, you probably know what I am talking about—the magazine man who would come to school assembly and offer you the world to sell magazine subscriptions.

There is simply nothing greater than getting to miss class to go to assembly when you're a kid. Assembly was usually a time where the school had something they had to teach all the kids about but didn't want to burden the teachers with it—so they would hire a company to come and teach us instead. The topics ranged on everything from reading, anti-bullying, and drug abuse awareness.

It was always a roll of the dice when you were told there would be an assembly, because you didn't know if it was going to be a D.A.R.E. officer trying to get you to not do drugs (by explaining to everyone exactly how to do drugs) or if it would be the yo-yo man. I loved the yo-yo man. In the school assembly world there is a definite hierarchy ranging from terrible to cool. The yo-yo man was close to the top: very cool. In the fourth grade we had a character-building assembly led by the yo-yo man that was about how you could be anything you wanted.

He would then sell yo-yos afterward, proving that you could be anything you wanted to be. Especially if you wanted to be a kid with a yo-yo and you had five dollars. I am happy to report that I won the fourth grade yo-yo contest that year. So dreams really do come true.

As great as the yo-yo man was, his fame paled in comparison to his excellency, the Weepul man. The Weepul man was really a magazine salesman, but he had all the charisma and voice of a gameshow host. He would open the assembly by announcing our school needed to raise money—and we could help make that happen while earning some pretty amazing prizes. Then he would remove the black sheet that was covering the sign announcing the bounty of prizes—and the gasps and cheers of the crowd went on for a full minute. We all sat there on the floor of the cafetorium enthralled with the possibility of earning a remote-control car, a Super Nintendo, or even the coveted trip to Disneyland!

Looking back now I realize that this was all a ploy to get kids to join a low-level pyramid scheme selling subscriptions of *Vogue* to our grandmothers who would never read them. However, at the time none of that mattered. Our eyes were on the prizes, and I wanted to win them all. The best part was that every day for two weeks we would start school with a twenty-minute assembly and every kid who'd sold magazines the night before would win a Weepul. What is a Weepul, you ask? Only the most unique adorable arts-and-crafts–looking prize on the planet. It was nothing more than a fluffy little pom-pom with googly eyes and foam feet—and yet they were a symbol of achievement and became the currency by which your elementary worth was determined for the next several weeks.

There was a never-ending supply of new Weepuls, as well. You may have earned the baseball player yesterday but today the Weepul man introduced the astronaut! I'm sure as much as we all loved the Weepul man, our parents must have hated him. Let's be honest, Mom and Dad were the real heroes of the operation. I was lucky for many reasons as a kid, one of which was that my mom owned a beauty salon and the one thing people love to do at a beauty salon, besides gossiping with their stylist, is read magazines. I cleaned up on the magazine sale. (Not so much during the World's Finest Chocolate sale, because all of my mom's friends were constantly dieting.)

One day I realized that the Weepul man had a pretty cool job. He got to show up and be a rock star, make people happy, and collect a paycheck. His energy and warmth encouraged and energized others. I didn't think about the monotony of doing the same spiel over and over or the wear and tear of travel or the fact that he really wanted to be an actor and this was his day job. I just knew that when I grew up, I wanted to be the Weepul man. Well, not really, I didn't want to sell magazines—I just wanted to make people happy.

At the end of the day, isn't that what we all want? We want to be the person who makes everyone else happy when we show up. We want to be the interesting person who came to the party. This isn't about being introverted or extroverted. It is about being seen as someone who adds value.

When I was a kid my parents loved the TV show *Cheers*. It is funny to think about all the shows I wasn't allowed to watch on account of them being inappropriate, but I could watch *Cheers* because they wanted to see it and we only had one TV. Most of the jokes went over my head but I still remembered them and laughed at them years later when I understood the context. The show was brilliantly written and had so many memorable characters; however, none of them stood out as much as Norm.

Often the show would start with Cliff telling Sam the bartender a long-winded story and all the patrons ignoring his rambling. Then out of nowhere the door would swing open and everyone would shout, "Norm!" We didn't know much about Norm or his life outside of this space. All we knew is that everybody loved Norm and, of course, we all want to go to a place where everybody knows your name.

Extra

THE WEEPUL MAN was my Norm, and I started doing everything I could to be the type of person others wanted to be around. There is a power in this way of being. You can actually shift the tone of the environment around you. I once heard someone mention an idea that is credited to Martin Luther King Jr. The basic thought is, as leaders, we need to be thermostats and not thermometers. A thermometer only reports the temperature but a thermostat actually changes the temperature.

In every environment we enter, we have the ability to bring up the tone of a room, to lighten the mood to make the experience better for everyone else. When others are hurting and feeling like they are alone, we can come around and encourage them. When messages of negativity and hopelessness are being shouted at our neighbors, we can be a voice of peace and positivity. This not only works in person but online as well.

It seems like once a week I see a friend post something like this on social media: "This platform is so full of nastiness and hate. I can't stand the fighting and negativity so I am deleting my account." I am not here to say I know what is best for anyone. Do whatever you need to do to stay healthy and in a good headspace. I have just chosen to take the route of sharing positivity and encouragement in this space—in person, on social media, and in all my communication. The more of us that do so, the better the whole place will be. There are no lone rangers in this effort, and there is always room for more Weepul people.

NoFuture Café

FROM THE TIME I was fifteen until I was eighteen, my Friday evening haunt was a little club in Pasadena, California, called NoFuture Café. This was one of the few local all-ages clubs and a hotspot of the local band scene. In the early '90s, Southern California had a booming community of local pop and punk bands. There was even a hotline you could call. It was really just the voicemail on some guy's pager that he updated every Wednesday night, listing the shows that were happening around town.

My buddies and I would call up the hotline on Wednesday and then plan our weekend. Thursday we might end up in the basement of a church in Arcadia watching a few hardcore bands. Saturday night we would often trek out to the O.C. to see some punk bands at Chain Reaction, and on Sunday it might be going to the Glass House in Pomona to see a more mainstream group like Weezer. While the locations tended to vary on the other nights, Fridays were strictly dedicated to NoFuture.

The set-up was simple: three dollars to see three bands and get all the iced mochas you could drink. At this time coffeehouses were big time. Nearly every coffeehouse had music at night, but it was usually folk or something very low key. At NoFuture, though, it was all about volume. *Loud and proud* was the motto. It was the kind of place that bands love to play, because everyone who came was ready for a show and they were true fans of music (or at least the free mochas, which were delicious).

I should probably mention that I, too, was in a band. We were called VBS, a name we happened upon completely by chance. Basically a few buddies from church and I got asked to play covers for a party, and while we were walking through the church building we saw a sign for the upcoming Vacation Bible School, and someone said, "What if we just call ourselves VBS?" We played the show, had a blast, and then someone said, "Why we don't become a real band?" Somehow the name stayed, and to this day I am embarrassed we didn't give it more thought.

We went from playing covers to writing original songs, and because we had been friends with so many bands in the scene, they started asking us to open for them. Some of my fondest memories of high school are playing shows with my buddies and dreaming of becoming real rock stars.

I remember our first paid gig. I was already performing magic at this time and had been booked to perform at the new McDonald's grand opening celebration on a Tuesday night. On a whim, I mentioned I had a band and we had quite the local following. The manager offered to have us play and then told me they could pay us a hundred dollars! We did the show and after we played for an hour the McDonald's folks said, "People are loving it, could you play another hour for another hundred bucks?" We didn't know any more songs but could play the same set again, we said. They agreed and we kept the party going.

Still on a high from our massive McDonald's success, we got a call from Aaron, the booker of NoFuture Café, telling us we had been booked! I was so excited and nervous to play at my favorite local club. The night of the show we were in the parking lot setting up. This club was so small that there was no green room or backstage. There was simply a door that opened on the stage that led to the parking lot. You would set up your gear outside and wait for your turn to go on. That night we were opening for a band called OZMA that later ended up touring with Weezer.

The setup for the bands was pretty cool. When people showed up they would say the name of the band they had come to see. After the first nine people, you would get one dollar for every person who said they were there to see you. Every member of our band went to a different school, which meant we had a lot of opportunity to get the word out with our homemade fliers. That first night at NoFuture we made $112 and had one of the greatest nights ever.

The best thing that happened at the club was when Katie and I went there on a date and I asked her if she wanted to be my girlfriend. I went the route of being super goofy and handed her a card that had conversation hearts glued to it in the phrase, "Will you be my girl-friend?" She said yes and we have been together ever since. I still can't believe I asked her out at a place called *NoFuture Café*. Against all odds and bad omens we have never left each other's side.

Extra

FOR A SEASON in my life this place was somewhere I could belong. Somewhere that affirmed creativity and dreams of the next generation. Long after the band played our last show, I still have incredible memories of this place that most of the week was an empty building but on Friday nights came alive as a safe refuge for young people who just needed somewhere to go and be themselves. It is where I learned about hospitality and making people feel welcome.

For many years Katie and I hosted a monthly break-fast at our house at which we would make an insane spread and invite people over for a time of good eats and encouragement. We would often have fifty or more people packed in our tiny living room and spilling out into the driveway. We took the idea of what NoFuture did with mochas and recreated it with omelets. What is something you could do for your coworkers or commu-nity to make them feel more welcome? How can we create an environment in our home and at our offices where people know we care? Let's try to take one step today to making our ordinary environments a little extraordinary.

Seeing the Signs

I WAS ONLY fifteen when I met the fetching Mrs. Hughes. Of course, at the time she was the fetching Katie Forster. We stood near each other in choir class (don't judge me), and I immediately took notice of her. She was beautiful in both body and spirit. She had a kind nature and joyful smile. We began hanging out with a small group of friends from choir, and we spent every spare moment together, so much fun in perfect four-part harmony. That last part may have been embellished.

It didn't take long before I knew that if I didn't end up with Katie, there must be another girl exactly like her somewhere. She was kind, so funny, a great friend, creative, pretty, and so humble. Having spent my entire life being around performers, it was refreshing to be around someone who didn't need to stand in the spot-light—and yet she still shone. (She doesn't like attention being put on her and there is a good chance she will never let these words be printed.)

Did I mention how funny she is? She is like a silent killer. She doesn't write down material like the rest of us hacks. You'll be in conversation and out of nowhere she will deliver a mic drop, comedy club closer that has everybody rolling. Someday I want to be that good and I am a "professional." My comedy is strictly a numbers game: say enough stuff and something will be funny. In high school I received the unfortunate title of 50/50 from one friend because my jokes only hit half the time. OK, enough about my shortcomings, back to the girl who said yes despite them.

Katie and I started dating in January of 1996. I tricked her into our first date by making her a card that said, "Please sign below to receive your birthday card." She signed in the box, which was actually a cutout in the front of the card. The inside read, "I agree to go on a date with Taylor" . . . followed by her freshly signed signature. I believe a similar technique was used by the United States during the Louisiana Purchase.

A few weeks later I asked her to be my girlfriend outside NoFuture Cafe with the conversation heart card. I was fifteen and even though she was a year older (high five) she said yes! Our relationship has always included doing simple but fun gestures to show how much we care.

A couple weeks later it was the morning of Valentine's Day and I was excited because I had planned a picnic lunch for us to have in the quad at school. I pulled up to school and Katie was standing there with her friend Stephanie. She had a big smile on her face, the kind you have when you've known about a secret and the other person is about to find out. "What's going on?" I asked. "Did you not see it?" she replied. "See what?" She immediately said, "Let's go" and we got in her car and headed toward my house.

That morning my mom was dropping me off and had taken a different route to the school to avoid traffic— which is why I hadn't seen Katie's surprise. And it was spectacular. Katie had been up before the sun rose to make and attach giant poster boards to huge trees in the center of the street we normally traveled down. As we drove past them, these massive billboards contained just one word each that spelled out: Taylor—Will—You—Be—My—Valentine?—Love—Katie.

I was overwhelmed once again by how great Katie was, that she would go this far to make sure I got the message. It was a truly wonderful moment. I started wondering what life would be like if I spent the rest of it with her. (Spoiler alert: It is incredible.) I wondered what kind of mischief we could create together. I wondered many things, but I didn't have to wonder if she cared. I knew that. *I saw the signs.*

Extra

WHAT COULD LIFE be like if we made sure that those we loved—our family, friends, neighbors—*knew.* If they didn't just hear us say that we cared, but instead there were signs that showed it. If we gave them something that cost us something. That day Katie posted the signs, I went back after school to get them and someone had taken them all except the ones that had our names. It is easy to give someone something that didn't cost you any time or money. It is also easy to blame others for missing the signs. I'm so glad that all those years ago Katie made sure I knew how she felt. I am even more grateful that over twenty years later we are still putting up signs.

A One Hundred–Gun Salute

WONDER BY ITS very nature can seem dangerous because it goes against the norm. If you are going to live your life chasing wonder, you can't expect to always be safe. Again, I am not encouraging recklessness, but I am encouraging a certain level of risk-taking. Nothing extraordinary ever began with just going with the flow. Adventure is always a little precarious and uncertain. My high school buddy Steve demonstrated this better than anyone.

Before Steve owned a car, he owned a boat. Once we were caught in a monsoon in the Grand Canyon and he ripped his shirt off to secure my twisted ankle and then got hypothermia and needed to be airlifted. That's another amazing story, but then again, every moment with Steve was wild. One summer morning when I was seventeen, Steve called me at 6:00 a.m. and said he was coming to pick me up for lunch. I asked why he would be picking me up so early for lunch and without joking at all, he said, "Because we are having lunch in Mexico!" And we did!

One of our greatest accomplishments when we were younger was the creation of our annual Fourth of July spectacular. It is important as I set the scene for you to know that my mother reminded me of this story just last night, and she herself questioned her parenting choices. In her defense, though, this was the time when, as a society, we were just starting to think of how to keep kids safe. In fact, our home city of Azusa was the only town nearby that allowed you to light fireworks on the Fourth. This made our house the perfect location for the spectacular to take place.

Steve and I improvised the first show, and it eventually became a yearly tradition. At our peak we had forty people in lawn chairs in my front yard, all of whom signed waivers to be there. We set up a PA system with a playlist that included everything from "God Bless America" to "Smells Like Teen Spirit." Once everyone was securely seated outside of the fire zone, Steve and I would make our entrance. We wore matching blue Dickies coveralls with American flag capes and a sparkler in each hand.

The show was a progression of pyrotechnics, starting with a series of fountains we leapt over and through. Then we used Roman candles to sword fight and even got the audience involved. One year a friend had planned to be part of the show but broke his leg during another adventure. This didn't stop us from making him the star: we hooked up some fountains to the back of his wheelchair and hurled him down the sidewalk to thunderous applause from the audience. In previous years this would have been the big finale, but this year we had a special surprise planned.

In the days leading up to the show, Steve was convinced that we needed to go bigger. Our reputation for this production had far exceeded our expectations, and we needed to give our deserving fans something unforgettable. I should have known we were in trouble when one day at lunch Steve started by saying, "So . . . I know this guy . . ." If your friend ever says something like that, just know whatever comes next is probably illegal. In this case it definitely was. I don't know how long the statute of limitations is on something like this, but just in case it hasn't passed, I cannot confirm or deny the rest of this story.

Steve said, "I know this guy who can get us the real fireworks." For our purposes here, "real fireworks" may or may not be "illegal fireworks." After lunch we told my mom we were heading to meet a guy who knew where we could get contraband pyro and she said, "Drive safe." Driving safe seems irrelevant if you are only driving to do a very dangerous activity, but nevertheless we were on our way.

We drove just a couple blocks away to a house I had never been to, and when we knocked on the door this towering figure opened it. He said, "What's up?" Steve then asked if his name was Hector. Hector replied with, "Yeah, the name's Hector, but you can call me the Block."

We asked Mr. The Block if he could tell us where to get some fireworks and he said, "Snitches get stitches," but if we drove him to the store so he could buy some beer with our money he would show us where to get them. Steve and I looked at each other then looked back at the Block and in unison said, "OK." After we drove him to the store, he gave us directions one street at a time until we came up to the place. He ran inside for what seemed like an eternity and just when we considered taking off, the garage door opened.

This was like the Toys "R" Us of illegal fireworks. Folding tables lined the walls and on each table there were boxes of the good stuff. Not a single package had any printed graphics, there were no eagles or American flags. Just brown craft paper packages with Sharpie-written names like "Doomsday" and "The Mother-in-Law." We surveyed the room before settling on the biggest one we could afford with what money we had left after the Block's beer run. It was called "The One Hundred–Gun Salute"!

Fast forward to the night of the big event and we had just sailed our newly injured friend down the street like a flaming bowling ball. We made the announcement: *For this last one, everyone needs to stand up.* Earlier in the evening we'd had a small accident and wanted everyone to be able to run if necessary. (We had found out that if you pinch a Piccolo Pete just right, it makes a crazy cool sound, but if you pinch a Piccolo Pete the wrong way, it will launch itself like a missile into the patio of the old folks' home across the street.)

So, everyone was standing at attention ready for the hundred-gun salute, and at this point we realized we had no instructions. We didn't know what this piece did or how it was gonna do it. The package was just brown paper, duct tape, a fuse, and the words "One Hundred–Gun Salute" written in Sharpie. We made the educated guess that the Sharpie side was the top. We lit it, ran away, and waited. For about thirty seconds nothing happened.

We were convinced we must have been taken for a ride, even though we had been driving. Apparently this guy had sold us a dud. Just as I began to apologize for the letdown, the loudest shotgun-sounding firework I have ever heard fired off and exploded a hundred feet above my parents' house. The crowd erupted with applause and fear. Then without warning, *boom!* it happened again, then *boom!* another. This proceeded to happen one hundred times! It really was a one hundred–gun salute.

Extra

WE COULD TALK all day long about how this was a bad idea, we could even talk all day long with the authorities. Again, I am not condoning or encouraging activity that could harm you or others. However, sometimes in life we play it so safe that we never live life to the fullest. I am a natural people pleaser: I want things to go well and I definitely don't want to let other people down. That way of thinking is great for keeping us safe, but it isn't so great for having adventures or finding new discoveries. We need friends who encourage chasing wonder in our personal lives—and in business we definitely need to surround ourselves with people who will challenge us to think outside of the norm. To help us become more creative.

In what area of your life have you been playing it too safe? Who are you worried about pleasing? Who is someone whose creativity both drives you and scares you a little? Again, we want to count the cost and make healthy decisions but healthy and safe aren't always on the same side. As I reexamine these stories with my buddy Steve, I am challenged to get back to a place where I had nothing to lose and everything to gain. To invite a little more play into my work life and to chase wonder . . . even if it means pushing the boundaries of what is considered safe or ordinary. Who knows what adventures are waiting on the other side of your fear? Let's be people who take action. Also, it's been a while since I connected with Steve. He is also married and has kids of his own; perhaps it is time I give him a call at 6:00 a.m. just to see if he wants to go get lunch!

Newlywed Nightmares

KATIE HAS BEEN the number one object of my affection since I was fifteen years old. I often say to her that I am the winner of all the boys because she chose me—and she laughs at my joking even though I am dead serious. My desire is that on my deathbed people won't talk about the shows I produced or the projects I created but instead will say, "He sure loved Katie."

Remember everything I just said when I begin to talk about all the things that went wrong when we first got married. Katie was twenty-two and I was twenty-one; at the time we felt like we'd waited so long to get married and now looking at the photos we were merely babies. I was working as a youth pastor at a large church and so the wedding invite list was massive. We had more than six hundred people attending and somehow the whole wedding cost less than six thousand dollars. This meant we did a lot of work on our own.

The day of the wedding I was climbing trees hanging paper lanterns for the reception up until about two hours before the ceremony. It is a weird feeling when you have been planning an event for months and the day actually arrives. On one hand you are stressed and hoping it goes well, on the other, you feel like it's out of your control at that point. The fact that Katie and I had spent nearly every day together for the last six years and had learned to laugh when things go wrong really prepared us for this day.

The audience had gathered in the church and I was walking in with the minister and my best man. You'll remember Steve from the fireworks spectacular. It was during this moment as we waited for the rest of the bridal party that Steve let me know he was really gassy. I encouraged him to just try and hold it in until after the most important day of my life. Everyone took their places and Katie was about to walk down the aisle.

Up until this exact moment I'd never enjoyed weddings. Even when good friends got married it all seemed so grand that I had a hard time connecting emotionally to the ritual. I would go to a wedding and it felt like I was watching a big production that felt kind of bizarre. That is, until the moment Katie walked down the aisle.

When I saw her enter the back of the church dressed in the most beautiful gown I had ever seen, I lost it. I didn't have a full-blown ugly cry, I was smiling and all, but massive tears of joy just started to pour down my face. I couldn't believe that this was my reality. That the girl of my dreams actually wanted to spend the rest of her life with me, and she was gonna stand in front of six hundred people and let them all know. How did I get this lucky?

It was at the peak of this realization that Steve farted. My best man, the guy who was there to ensure this day was perfect, broke wind on stage as my bride was making her grand entrance. This continued throughout the ceremony, but Steve's aggressive crop dusting was not the most awkward moment of the ceremony. That happened when the minister mentioned that the first time he saw Katie show up with her blonde hair and bright blue eyes he thought, *Who is this little Nazi?* Yes, the minister called Katie a Nazi on our wedding day! I have the very expensive wedding video to prove it.

We survived the ceremony and headed to the reception. Now the post-nuptial party is always a little hectic but with six hundred attendees who all wanted to talk to us, we were exhausted and didn't even get to eat. Later that night we drove off to the first stop on our weeklong honeymoon. We wanted to save money and go somewhere we could visit regularly in the future, so we chose to take a trip up the California coast. Our first stop would be two nights in Dana Point, which was only about an hour away but at the end of a long day and my being excited to get to our destination, it seemed like an eternity.

We were ten minutes away from the hotel when the car stopped working. Apparently in our hurried preparations for the ceremony I forgot to fill up the car with gas. That's right! I ran out of gas on my wedding night—wait that didn't sound right. The *car* ran out of gas. You know what I mean. Luckily we were able to coast off the freeway and right into a gas station, saving me at least a little of embarrassment. Our dinner that evening consisted of a bottle of water and some Pringles I bought at the gas station, since all the restaurants were closed.

We arrived at the resort after midnight and waited outside for fifteen minutes before someone came to let us in. To say that this is not the fairy-tale experience we imagined would be an understatement. However, I wouldn't change a thing. Maybe having more gas in the car and less gas in my best man, but that's it. The reality is so many people are worried about giving the illusion of having everything be perfect. I would rather laugh through the chaos with someone I love than have a perfect wedding video that no one will ever want to see anyway.

Our newlywed life continued to be a little crazy. We were so young! Katie had never lived outside of her parents' house and I'd moved out six months earlier only because we found the apartment we wanted. It was this little duplex that my dad actually lived in when my parents split up. I know that sounds kind of weird but I had wonderful memories of staying in this place every other week as a kid. One time my dad brought me some snap poppers that were like mini-firecrackers with strings you would pull to make them pop. I would always tie their little green and white strings to the door knobs and try to scare my dad. When Katie and I moved in to the place sixteen years later, there were still strings tied to all the doorknobs.

Being newly married and also moving out for the first time was great because we got to learn how to adult together . . . and we made tons of mistakes. One embarrassing thing is that when I lived at home there were always people around so for the six months I lived alone before our wedding, I never wore pants at home. I got so used to just walking into the house and immediately taking off my pants. About two weeks after we got home from our honeymoon, we had some friends over for dinner and a movie. Ten minutes into the movie, without fully realizing we had company, I stood up and took off my pants.

About a year later we were able to buy our first condo. It was 687 square feet, and we were so proud of having our own place! It even had a dishwasher, which was a big deal, because when I was a kid we always just washed dishes in the sink. I was feeling so proud of our new place, and I decided I was going to load the dishwasher. Katie and I then sat down to watch TV, which was just around the corner from the kitchen. (Of course, this place was so small that everything was just around the corner from the kitchen.) This is when I first learned that there is a difference between dish soap and dishwasher soap. Out of the corner of my eye I saw this four-foot wall of foam that had overtaken the kitchen and was working its way into the living room. We cleaned up the mess but never forgot the memory.

Extra

LOOKING BACK AT all these times things went wrong, I am grateful that Katie and I were in the mess together. I am grateful that we never took ourselves too seriously, that we laughed then knowing that it would be funny later. Even now—after nineteen years of marriage and two kids—we still make mistakes. Every day we have to laugh about another thing that went wrong. It is a good reminder that we aren't perfect. That we are still learning.

Fairy-tale endings are boring. Remember if someone tries to act like they have it all together, they do not. Let's not fall into the comparison trap of thinking that everyone else's life is picture-perfect and ours isn't. Life is messy for all of us. When I was a kid and I came home dirty from school, my mom didn't get mad, she just assumed it was a good day. The next time your day gets a little messier than you expected, try to give yourself the same grace.

For the Love of Old Things

I HAVE ALWAYS been interested in the past. Specifically in items connected to the past. This most certainly started with my parents, as they both have a love of antiques. The house I grew up in was built in 1901 so even it was an antique! My mom's love of vintage items manifested itself in collecting furniture. The number of times she would come home from work with a dresser or chair that she found are too many to count. She just couldn't stand seeing something like that be thrown away.

My dad's love of old stuff was all related to pop culture and cars. He loved Coca-Cola memorabilia and at one time owned nearly everything that ever had that logo on it. We would cruise in his 1954 Chevy to the local drive-in movie theater, where they would hold a massive swap meet every Sunday. The swap meet was a magical place for me. You could find everything under the sun and you got the feel that every person there appreciated old stuff just like you.

As we walked Dad would say, "Do you know what this is?" He would then explain to me that it was a tissue box holder you could mount under the dash of your car, or that the gramophone was one of the first ways that recorded music was enjoyed. There would always be an

E-Z Up canopy with a couple of tables that had cheap toys for sale. While all of the other kids flocked there, I would convince my dad to let me buy a vintage one-piston toy steam engine. I would take the stuff home, take it apart to see how it worked, and then learn how to reassemble it.

My dad made me feel like I didn't have to be afraid to take something apart, because you could always put it back together. I grew up at a time when safety was less of a concern and a wood-burning kit was still a very reasonable gift for a nine-year-old. Once my dad taught me how to make a hot dog cooker. We got a wood board and nailed two nails slightly further apart than the length of a hot dog. Then he used pliers to bend the sharp ends of the nails toward one another, so you could suspend the hot dog between the two nails. Next he took an old extension cord from a lamp and wrapped each wire around one of the nails. You simply plug it in and the hot dog gets fried. I realize this is incredibly dangerous—but it also taught me to not be afraid of experimentation. Not to mention I had the perfect opportunity to shout out to the neighborhood, "IT'S ALIVE!"

I love finding ways to make old things serve a new purpose. I started collecting old speakers and hooked them into my stereo to see how differently each one sounded. One time my dad brought me home an old Rain Bird sprinkler controller. It was a lockable metal box and inside were dozens of switches. I ended up hooking up the switches so that they turned the different speakers on and off. I realize this is pretty nerdy, but I absolutely loved it.

When Katie and I started dating in high school we realized how much we both loved old things. While other couples went on dates to the mall, we would go antique or thrift store shopping. To this day we are constantly finding new ways to utilize old things. I love that our house is a collection of items that other people discarded and Katie transformed with her amazing design ability. In fact, our house was built in 1906, so we are keeping that tradition alive too.

Katie has even created a business of finding old furniture pieces and giving them new life. She is able to see things others view as past their prime and recreates them in a way that they can be loved and enjoyed for years to come. She adores history and will look at an old cabinet and imagine who had this in their home and how much they took pride in it. It really is amazing to know that these pieces will go on to live another hundred years because of the care she puts in them.

As of late I have a new appreciation for old coins. My mom has a coin collection and has always looked at her pocket change to see if there are any hidden gems in there. I use a few coins for a magic routine and one of them is a silver dollar from 1879. It amazes me every time I hold it. I am reminded of my mortality in an interesting way. It is a bizarre feeling to hold something in your had that has been around longer than anyone on the planet and will most likely outlive all of us as well. That coin could have been used as bail to buy someone's freedom, or it could have been used as a bribe to take advantage of others.

Extra

THESE OLD ITEMS are a reminder to me of the time we possess. Time is a gift. It existed before us and will go on after us. We are merely keepers of it momentarily. What we choose to do with our time can build others up or tear them down. It is our responsibility to make the most of the limited time we have. I have always enjoyed the biblical analogy that our life is like a vapor—it appears for a moment and then vanishes. We should live every day attempting to add a little extra to the ordinary that is our lives. Let's create stories and things that future generations will value, and that will bring more life to those with whom we share this brief moment of time.

Parenting Fails

WHEN I WAS a kid I thought parents had it easy. They get to make all the decisions, no one tells them when to go to bed, and they can have ice cream whenever they want. Sadly, I thought this up until the very moment I became a parent. Katie and I both knew we wanted kids and that we wanted them while we were still young. I didn't want to be an old dad. Every class had a kid with an old dad. The guy who built his career empire only to settle down and start having kids when he was in his fifties. When I was eight my friend Ben's dad was in his late sixties! We all knew it was strange, but we also couldn't talk about it.

Katie got pregnant just two years after we got married, and we were so excited to be parents. When our first, Maddy, was ready for her big debut, we were at the hospital anxious for her arrival. Katie decided to try to forgo pain medication because she had been told it would slow down the labor. She would rather just tough it out, she thought. Well, after ten hours of labor without meds the doctor told us that the umbilical cord was wrapped around her and we needed to do a C-section. Katie immediately screamed, "Get me the anesthesiologist!" Our sweet Maddy Rose arrived and for the first time we started to feel the weight of reality. Maddy was born on August 20, and our anniversary is August 23. That morning Katie and I woke up from probably two minutes of sleep total, and looking at each other completely exhausted, we said simultaneously, "Happy anniversary."

A few minutes later the nurse came in and said we were ready to go home. At this point I realized I was not ready to go home. The first few days of parenting are spent in the hospital, where you have a false sense of confidence in your abilities, because you forget there is an entire crew of people helping keep you and the baby alive. Every couple of hours someone brings you a sandwich and some Jell-O. Also, there is a magical diaper drawer that they refill like a bottomless drink at Chili's.

I spent about an hour installing the car seat in the car—which, by the way, no one tells you how to do. I then had to drive my wife, who was recovering from major surgery, and the new human we were just allowed to *leave* with, home in our little SUV. I was more nervous getting on that freeway than the first time I learned to drive. Hands at ten and two all the way home. After about a week of our trying to figure out parenting, Katie looked at me, exhausted again, and said, "How is it that every parent does this? Is this actually what having a baby is like?"

I don't for a second want you to think that having a baby isn't the most wonderful thing in the world, because it absolutely is. It's just really, really hard to be a parent. It is an incredibly humbling experience and a lesson in being OK with being out of control. When I was a kid I thought parents had it all under control. The reality is they were just making it up one step at a time and doing the best they could do.

As a parent you learn to think on your toes real quick. Plans are constantly having to change and you have to be able to roll with the punches. One time we had planned a trip to the zoo when out girls were five and three years old. We planned it a few weeks in advance and the kids were so excited. I had also played it up a lot, so when the big day came, we were prepared. We brought lunches, maps, and a list of all the animals we wanted to see.

For whatever reason, though, this was the day *none* of the animals decided to show up for work. We went by the lions and they were all in their little den. The birds were nesting, the elephants had been moved somewhere out of sight so the zoo could work on their habitat. It was the worst zoo visit ever. So we cut our zoo day short. Meanwhile, I had two crying kids in car seats and a disappointed wife looking at me wondering, *What we are gonna do now?*

I thought for a while. Where could I take them where they could see animals for sure? Then the solution hit me: *Bass Pro Shop.* Those of you who have ever been to Bass Pro, you know this to be a terrible idea, but for those of you who haven't, I will just say they have quite a collection of animals . . . in a wide variety of poses . . . on display . . . thanks to the wonders of taxidermy. Now, I thought this would be educational . . . and for the first part of the trip the kids were really excited and completely thrilled.

The kids started with gasps of "Wow!" and "Look how pretty!" pointing in every direction as new animals were being discovered. Soon enough, though, Kennedy suddenly paused, took a beat, and then asked why none of them were moving. I had to think fast. I quickly explained to her that these animals were retired. That when they died people stuffed them and placed them here so we could appreciate and learn about them. This seemed to do the trick and the girls started to get excited again. "Did that used to be a deer?" "Did that used to be a bobcat?" We had done it! The kids were seeing animals.

Everything was going great, and I was ready to give myself the Father-of-the-Year award, until we walked into the junior women's clothing section and Maddy saw a mannequin, then screamed, *"Did that used to be a real girl?"*

Extra

THIS IS JUST one of the many stupid mistakes we have made as parents. Nearly every day Katie and I question whether we are making the right decisions for our girls. Any parent who is doing the best for their kids will always wonder if they could have done more. Just know that if you are taking the approach of wanting to do what is best for them, you may make tons of mistakes but you aren't failing as a parent. Your kids will know you love them because of the effort, not the outcome. So go out there and fail extraordinarily.

Talking to Your Eight-Year-Old Self

OFTEN IN LIFE we find ourselves asking, *What is next?* It is very easy to get stuck in the idea of not knowing where we should head next or what moves to make. We read books to inspire us, troll social media to see what other people are doing, even ask for a sign from heaven to show us a guiding light. When I find myself trapped in one of these moments, I make an appointment with a friend who knows me better than anyone and has never let me down—my eight-year-old self.

Eight is a great year. You are old enough to understand that life is different than you originally thought, but you are still a kid. You have the perfect balance of reality and imagination. As we get older that pendulum tends to swing hard toward reality because we are faced with it daily. From the moment you wake up the world is shouting reality at you. It's hard to avoid. In fact, we are conditioned to immediately ask what the current reality is. We feel the need to get caught up. Within ten minutes of our eyes being opened each morning, we have checked the news, checked Twitter, and then scrolled our friends' social media pages to see what each of their individual realities are.

We are faced with more reality every day than many

of our ancestors experienced in a lifetime. We have forgotten how much whimsy, wonder, and imagination were supposed to be a part of our approach to life. This is why you should regularly schedule appointments with your eight-year-old self. Back then you didn't have life all figured out and you knew it, and that is a great jumping-off point. Today we think we have it all figured out. We have instant access to all human knowledge, and so we feel terrible when there are seemingly no answers to the problems we face.

There is a reason that shows like *Kids Say the Darndest Things* make us laugh. It is because kids tell it to you straight. They haven't been so socially conditioned to be worried about your ego. They are so much more honest than adults! It's been amazing watching my daughters grow up, because they have this innocent common sense that many adults lack. Things like treating others the way you want to be treated seem so obvious to them while we "mature" adults are still trying to figure that out.

The great thing about talking to your eight-year-old self is that you know when you're full of it. You will call baloney on yourself when others might give you a break or have sympathy for your poor excuses. There is a saying that you are your own worst critic. I agree that the current you *is* your worst critic, but your eight-year-old self can be your strongest ally.

Extra

SO WHAT DOES an appointment with your kid self look

like? For me it is simple. I just ask, "What would eight-year-old me think of this?" In times when I have been a little ungrateful, my eight-year-old self reminds me of how much I would have given for this opportunity. If I'm going one of two ways on a decision, I let kid me decide. When I am working too much, my eight-year-old self says, "Go spend time with your family." Also, my kid self is very impressed that Katie married me.

This is the closet thing to time travel I have ever experienced. We are all servants of time. We cannot undo the past or see into the future, but we all have the ability to view our current circumstance through the eyes of a child. Remember, the day you are living today is the day you dreamed about years ago. This time right now is what you looked forward to. Go back in time and let the child in you drive for a while today. You will take yourself on a great adventure and will be a better human because of the experience.

Magical Mishaps

As I LEARNED very early on with the milk trick at Shannon's birthday party, magic tricks don't always go as planned. Anyone who has spent a life in show business will tell you that anything that *can* go wrong, will. I thought that on-stage humiliation would be something I would grow out of over time. The sad truth is if you do anything 250 times a year, it is probably gonna not always go perfectly. Here are a few of my favorite moments of magician mishaps.

Ever since I heard that there was a magic club whose clubhouse was a castle in Hollywood, I was committed that I would one day be a part of the Magic Castle. The Magic Castle is the premier magic destination in the world and the home to the Academy of Magical Arts. It began in the early 1960s when two brothers, Bill and Milt Larsen, created a magic wonderland of their own. Ever since its inception, the Castle has been an exclusive evening out and is often the host to A-list celebrities who appreciate the strict no photography policy and upscale dressy vibe.

I first heard of the club while at my local magic shop. I found out that although you need to be twenty-one to become a member, they had a junior society where budding young magicians could learn their craft and participate in monthly meetings—at the Castle! I was thirteen, which was just old enough to audition, so I filled out my application and rehearsed a five-minute act to present at the biannual audition. On the big day I waited nervously for my chance to perform and even more nervously for the letter to arrive a few weeks later saying that... I didn't get in. Not many people know this but it took me three auditions to make it into the club. It also took me three tries to get my driver's license, but that isn't what we are talking about right now.

The third time I auditioned I was seventeen years old and my skills as a performer were much better than they were the first two times I had come through. I was prepared and I knew it. I stood behind the curtain with a deck of cards already out of the box and ready for my flourish filled opener. When they called my name I burst through the curtains with such momentum that the cards escaped my grip and went fluttering down to the ground. To this day I cannot remember what I said, but apparently the joke was good. When I received my acceptance letter, the leadership said that it was my ability to recover from that mistake and to use humor as a cover that showed them I had the appropriate level of skill.

Less than six months later it was time to audition for the yearly Future Stars show. This was the one week out of the year that junior magicians could be featured in the evening showrooms for a week—and you even got paid! Katie—who was my girlfriend at the time—had been assisting me with my first big illusion, Houdini's meta-morphosis. This is a classic illusion where the magician is tied into a bag and placed in a locked trunk, the assistant stands on top and throws up a cloth. Moments later the two have switched places. We were doing a comedy version where we switch places so quickly that she is now wearing my shirt and tie and I am left wearing her sparkly top. However, for the Castle I wanted to add something more impressive and escape from regulation police handcuffs at the same time.

I recently discovered a way to make it look and sound like you are being locked up with real handcuffs and then you can escape. I used this at a restaurant on an off-duty police officer and ended up getting my meal paid for. When it works it is pretty great . . . but on the day of our big audition, it did not work. Both Katie and I were anxious to be performing on the legendary Palace of Mystery stage at the Castle in front of our peers and several legendary performers. We started the routine and it was going smoothly until Katie put the handcuffs on and gave me a look of terror. She'd accidentally locked me up for good and we didn't have an extra key in the trunk. Not knowing what to do she continued on, looked me in the eye and slowly closed the lid on me.

I ended up getting out but not without a massive bruise from ripping my hand through the partially closed cuff. That same day we went to leave and realized we had thrown all of our personal items—including the car keys—in the magic trunk before we locked it. A good business move would have been to have a spare key, but we learned that lesson the hard way. *Interesting fact: the trick is made to get out of but not to break into.* I could share horror stories for days. One time we had Katie secretly loaded into a larger-than-life prop "dollhouse" and as my friend Steve was rolling the antique illusion onto the stage behind me, one of the wheels got caught in a crack and the leg snapped right off. Everyone in the audience gasped. Without missing a beat, I looked straight at the audience and said, "For my next routine . . ." and quickly moved on as Steve continued dragging the now tilted dollhouse with Katie in it off into the wings as if *that* was the way it was meant to be. Ah, live theater!

Probably my favorite mishap of all was when we were performing a huge show as a fundraiser for the Boy Scouts at a huge Catholic church auditorium. We were doing a full ninety-minute show with an intermission and large-scale illusions. We worked out a cool variation of our metamorphosis trick, in which Katie would go into the box and I would stand on top. The cloth would fly up and when it came down Katie was outside and inside the locked trunk was the emcee. I would then be in the back of the room. It was a really cool routine.

Whenever we did this routine, I would have to find the best secret path to the back of the room from backstage so that once I escaped I could get into position as quickly as possible. Since we performed this in different venues each night, I would need to find the most direct route for that venue. We got there early in the day to set up, then rehearsed, and found an absolutely perfect passage through a hallway that led from the stage to the back of the room. Once the show started and the house lights were down, Katie noticed that whenever that door to the hallway opened, light flooded the room and people turned and looked. This would have ruined the surprise of my appearance. So while I was on stage Katie simply locked the door and wrote a sign that said, "You have to find another way."

I was giving my closing remarks on stage before the finale and there was no way for her to talk with me. So needless to say, once I escaped and read the sign on the locked door I freaked out. I had exactly fifty-two seconds to find a new way. I left out the backstage door and ended up in the parking lot. Not knowing what to do I started running around the building. I ran into the first entrance and interrupted a prayer group. I yelled, "So sorry!" then continued on my journey. I eventually ran through the entrance and had to explain the reason I didn't have a ticket was because it was *my show* and I had to be in there *right now*! I ran through the lobby and into the doors two seconds before Katie pointed, revealing I was in the back of the room. Huge applause from the audience and none the wiser that I had just run my very first unplanned marathon. Whew!

Extra

SURVIVING MOMENTS LIKE these not only make for great stories, but they help make it a little easier the next time something goes wrong. Perhaps you are at a moment right now in which you were heading one direction and the door you thought was going to open for you was closed. It doesn't mean you won't reach that goal. You just need to find another way. Mistakes happen, but don't let that keep you from chasing wonder and experiencing the real magic of life.

Odd Mall Jobs

THERE ARE THREE times in my life that I worked at the mall, and every time was a complete disaster. When you are starting out in the entertainment business, every opportunity sounds amazing and most of them aren't, which means you end up with a lot of great stories. When I was twenty, one of my first big opportunities was to perform trade-show magic for a bank that had a kiosk in the mall. My job was basically to draw a crowd, weave the company's message into my show, and then get them to talk to one of the employees about opening a savings account.

I enjoyed the *idea* of this job more than the actual work itself. Up to this point I had primarily been performing for local birthday parties and the occasional business Christmas party. The idea of doing trade-show magic seemed like such a relief from the chaos I was used to. What I didn't realize is that these shows were just as chaotic and twice as exhausting. I would basically do the same fifteen-minute presentation twice an hour for eight hours. Toward the end of the day I would have a hard time remembering if I'd already told a joke or showed a magic trick to the same group of people.

I really wanted to impress the agent who booked me

and the client as well so the pressure was on, but that wasn't as stressful as what happened to me next. One Saturday about three weeks in to this gig I arrived at the mall early. Other than the group of older women who walked before the mall opened, it was basically a ghost town. I got to the booth and tucked my performance case under a skirted table, then went to use the restroom. When I got back to set up about thirty minutes before my first set, my case was gone.

I looked all around the booth and then I began running frantically through the mall. First of all, I cherished that case. It was an ATA flight case, the type of expensive road case musicians use to protect their equipment. Something you should know about magicians is that we love luggage. I could spend hours looking for the perfect suitcase. And there are so many questions that need to be answered, like how light is it? Will it hold up to rain, snow, and aggressive airline baggage handlers? Will all of my props safely fit along with my clothes and personal items? The search for the perfect suitcase is a bizarre side effect of having to pack constantly. Most importantly, *that* particular suitcase had everything in it I needed to perform my show for the next eight hours straight.

After combing the mall and not seeing anyone who might have taken it, I burst into the security office frantically and said, "Someone has stolen my case!" The security guards looked immediately concerned and asked me to describe the case. They then walked me out to the empty parking lot where another security guard was standing about a hundred feet away from it. My case! But this was just after September 11, 2001, and security had seen a man (me) in a dark suit walk in with an intense-looking black briefcase, hide it before the mall opened, and leave. They thought that I had planted a bomb. The bomb squad was on their way to investigate. Imagine how bad they would have felt if their bomb robot opened it only to find two decks of playing cards, sixteen oranges, and a fake thumb.

My second appearance at the mall was when I got hired to perform the grand opening of the new fitness gym. I wasn't getting paid money, but I had negotiated for both Katie and I to get free memberships for the first five years. I was told they were holding a huge extravaganza—there would be a theater set up and we would be performing in front of five hundred people at a time.

This seemed like a good opportunity for some big exposure—a phrase I later learned meant the same as no money. Because there would be a huge stage and crowd, Katie and I decided we would perform a few of our grand illusions. We rented a trailer, set up the props at home, and then went through the trouble of getting these giant set pieces up to the second floor where we would be performing. When we arrived, there was no crowd other than the half dozen other performers who had arranged similar deals. There was also no stage, which meant that I ended up sawing my wife in half next to people in line to buy pretzels and angry gym customers who just wanted to work out. Oh, and by the way, during our entire five-year membership, we went a total of three times. Feel the burn!

Both of these situation pale in comparison to the worst job I ever agreed to do that also just happened to be at the mall. There is a word for a young newly married youth pastor who also moonlights as a magician, and that word is *poor*. The amount of times I overdrew my bank account just to have enough money to buy lunch meat and tortillas was ridiculous. However, if you tasted Katie and I's signature dish, the ham, cheese, and barbecue sauce wrap, you would see why it was worth going into debt over. All this to say, some of the gigs I took were because they brought me joy and others were because I was desperately broke.

My sister Cheri was a rising star at a youthful clothing brand store in the mall, the type of place that cranked techno music and you could smell their signature cologne all the way across the food court. She told me that she needed to hire a DJ for an event at their store and wondered if, since I had a great PA system, I wanted to do it. It was only for four hours and she would pay me $250. I didn't want to do it but I thought it would be good quality time with my sister, and … who am I kidding? I did it for the money.

The day of my big MC debut I showed up early to the store to get set up. Upon arrival I met Leo, one of the store managers, who told me that Cheri was off today but that he would help me. My sister happened to leave out the small detail that I would be flying solo. I spent about forty-five minutes setting up my speakers, running cables out of sight, and taping everything down so that it looked great and would be safe for the customers. Fifteen minutes before the doors opened, Leo said he didn't like where it was in the corner and asked if I could move to the middle of the store where everyone could see me.

I was not excited about being on display, but I did what he asked and soon was sweating profusely from moving tons of gear in a hurry. The store opened and the looks I received from the young shoppers were fierce. They looked at me like *this guy looks like a youth pastor*, which I was at the time, but it still hurt. Leo then said, "And of course you play any songs that customers request?" I agreed, thinking the chances of that happening were slim to none. Then people started coming up requesting songs. This was years before services like Spotify, so I spent a small fortune, way more than the gig was paying, buying songs online to keep the customers happy.

I ended up putting the playlist on shuffle, told my sister I just wasn't cut out for this job, and left my gear there out of embarrassment until the mall closed. These were just a few of the many gigs from hell that I never should have said yes to.

Extra

PART OF THE learning process is realizing that you don't have to say yes to every opportunity. It isn't that I was better than these shows, it was simply that there were people more qualified than me to fulfill that position.

While it was embarrassing to find myself having to do something that I wasn't a good fit for, I am so glad that I learned this early on in my career. Now when an opportunity comes up, I don't just say yes. Even if I really want to do it. I think about if it is a good fit for me and the client. Sometimes I have to be honest and tell them their project isn't where my gifting lies. While it can be disappointing to give up really cool things like TV appearances with celebrities, I have found it is just as exciting to call up a friend who I know will knock it out of the park and give them the recommendation.

There is a temptation in life to take everything that comes your way out of fear that another opportunity won't come. I have learned that extraordinary opportunities will become an ordinary occurrence if you are honest with who you are. The more you get in tune with what you are good at, the more other people will recognize it and feel comfortable giving you the chance. So ask yourself this question: What is the one thing I do that I can do better than most people? What are the things that bring me the most joy? Find the intersection of those two questions and you will find your opportunities.

Fire and Ice

I GREW UP going to church, and some of my fondest memories are the time I spent attending youth group activities. Youth group is a funny place, it's kinda like church but a whole separate thing. As a kid I got the idea that the church wanted to meet but didn't want the parents to be worried about their kids so they made this other thing for us to go to—which was great because it meant we didn't have to go to "Big People Church." Also, because it was run by volunteers, all of the leaders were young adults who'd just graduated out of this program a few years before. It's crazy to me that I was allowed to go on trips out of state and even out of the country that were organized by some twenty-two-year-olds just trying to make it all work.

The summer I was going into high school my family gave the youth group permission to kidnap me and take me to a Denny's restaurant as a form of initiation. About twenty-five people came into my room to wake me up at 7:00 a.m. I am so glad that this was not the day I tried out sleeping naked! Before we went to breakfast they took me to Walmart and had me stand up in a shopping cart and use a raft oar to push myself through the parking lot singing "Row, row, row your boat" as they filmed the whole thing. It was a blend of excitement and terror and I am an extrovert. I can't image how many people were scarred by a similar story that I look upon with fondness.

Youth groups activities were always stacked about 95 percent fun and 5 percent Bible lesson, which felt like the perfect balance to me. Apart from attending the Sunday morning large group meeting, we would have a Wednesday night group that met at my home with just about seven other guys my age. It was a great chance to be able to talk about stuff going on with the family and at school and to just feel like I wasn't alone with my thoughts. While I would later become a pastor and eventually leave the church all together over some pretty disheartening experiences, I would not trade my time in youth group to this day.

I loved being there so much that when I graduated high school I decided to stick around and volunteer with the junior high kids. You had to wait at least a year before coming back to work with the high school students. Looking back it seems crazy to let a nineteen-year-old be a leader to high school students. Each week I would help set up for the Sunday morning service, hang out with kids before and after the program started, and help lead small group breakout discussions. Within a few weeks of volunteering they announced that we would be holding our next all-nighter and I couldn't wait.

Much to my parents' dismay, I offered up our house as the location for about fifteen junior high boys and six volunteer leaders to stay up all night eating junk food and creating a combination of body odor that would not leave our house for three weeks afterward. The plan was to have a series of activities throughout the city from about 5:00 p.m. Friday until 10:00 p.m., and then do a movie marathon at my folks' house until the students were picked up early Saturday morning. This being the first time I was one of the leaders planning an event, I wanted it to be memorable—but it ended up being unforgettable.

After grabbing some food, we went to the local grocery store. This was the only store that had the very unique item we were looking for, ten-pound blocks of ice. We bought one for each student and then headed to a park about twenty minutes away that had the largest grass hill around. The whole time, students were asking "Where are we going? What are we doing?" We told them it was a surprise but it would be worth it. We all lined up on top of this hill and had everyone fold up a beach towel until it was the size of the block of ice. We then placed the towels on the ice blocks, sat on them, and sailed at an aggressive speed down the massive grassy mountainside. About halfway down there was a sidewalk that ran through the hill. This made a sort of jump as you crossed the sidewalk and landed on the hard block of ice on the other end.

The look on the guys' faces was priceless. Growing up in California, this was as close to snow sledding as many of them had ever seen. I had done this years ago when I was a kid and was shocked to find out that none of these students had ever done it before. And then I found out it had apparently become illegal since the first time I had tried it. The sun was setting and at the top of the road opposite the park, a police car was shining his lights on all of us. The youth pastor told everyone to pack up and get in the cars. I was driving my mom's minivan and a bunch of kids piled in. As all three vehicles were pulling out of the parking lot, the police officer entered the parking lot and turned on his siren.

I had just turned right out of the parking lot and pulled over waiting for the inevitable. The youth pastor, our trusty leader, turned left, and the officer decided to follow him. I was both relieved and afraid of what would happen with the other guys so I followed at a distance and pulled into a grocery store parking lot across the street as the officer pulled them over. It turns out one of the kids still had a baseball-sized piece of ice in his hand and threw it out the window as the policeman was tailing them. The officer thought they were tossing drugs, and the next forty minutes of watching the youth pastor sweat and have to walk the line was pretty great. I was just grateful it wasn't me.

We then all went to pick up a few dozen donuts at our favorite local spot before heading to the "witch's house." Did I mention that we had no business leading youth? There was a lady in our neighborhood who either was—or wanted everyone to think she was—a witch. She had blacked out the street light in front of her house with a trash bag and spray-painted ominous warnings on her garage door. We thought it would be a good idea to challenge one of the guys to go knock on her door. What he *didn't* know was that another one of the cars had arrived early and was waiting to scare him. The more of this story I type, the more I realize this was a counterintuitive activity for an organization trying to help people emotionally and spiritually.

Late in the evening we headed back to my parents' house. I was exhausted and it wasn't even eleven o'clock. I was beginning to rethink the whole idea of volunteering. Meanwhile the kids were explaining a game in which someone yells "Fire drill!" at a red light and everyone jumps out and runs around the car before getting back in. I picked up on their conversation at the same time I noticed a police car in my rearview mirror. We were only two blocks away from my parents' house, and I found myself dreaming that within a few minutes I would be relaxing on the couch and decompressing from the night's adventurous activities. As we drove toward the next intersection, the light turned red and I promptly stopped the car. That is when one of the boys yelled "Fire drill!" at the top of his lungs.

Before I could stop them, the van doors flew open and a dozen or more junior high boys poured into the street like it was a clown car. I just watched it all unfold in slow motion. The pandemonium was insane. Kids were running around in every direction. The only one left in the car . . . was me. To this day I cannot explain why I did what I am about to tell you. Maybe it was delirium, maybe it was survival instinct. I do know it was incredibly stupid, but for some reason, I floored it. That's right . . . at a red light, with a policeman behind me and with kids running in the street past curfew, I blew through that light like the start of a drag race.

I drove the two blocks to my parents' house, got out, and stood in front of the car to see the kids running after me down the street and the police officer with sirens blazing, shining the searchlights back in forth. The students all lined up along the van one by one without saying a word, as if they, too, had just realized the gravity of the situation and were practicing the look for their mug shots. We sat there silently as the police officer pulled up slowly in front of the house. He rolled down his window, saw the fear in our eyes, shook his head and drove away.

This story is chock-full of stupid decisions. One major takeaway for me is while I disagree in hindsight with many of my decisions and realize how much worse the situation could have been, the heart behind it all was good. I wanted to be there for these guys when other people weren't. I wanted them to know they weren't alone. I wanted them to have crazy fun and make memories. In the process I made a lot of stupid mistakes. When you try to help people, you will mess up. You will make mistakes, but don't let that stop you from helping people.

I love those moments when people don't have all the answers but they still try to help others. The truth is, in life, we spend so much time trying to do all the right things, trying to have the right answer for every situation. But have you ever gotten caught in a moment where you weren't prepared and you screwed up completely?

I want to tell you a personal story about my sister. My

sister, Sara, is a tall, amazing woman. And one day in college, she went to a 7-Eleven to get something to drink. She chose her cup and was about to get a fountain drink. It was a hot day and she was hanging with some friends in Simi Valley, California. As she made a beeline straight for the fountain she heard, "Excuse me." She looked around. There was no one behind her, no one beside her. She didn't know what was going on. She thought, *Maybe I'm just hearing things.* Again she began to fill the fountain drink and heard "Excuse me," one more time.

She looked down and there, just below the soda fountain, stood Verne Troyer, the actor who played Mini-Me in the Austin Powers movies. A great actor, hilarious guy, and a super sweet dude that day, because here's what happened. Verne grabbed a cup, held it up to my sister, and said, "Would you help me?" This is the point at which most of us would say, "Absolutely. I'm honored. Huge fan of your work, love your movies. What can I get you?" Then get a cup and help him out. Not my sister, no. She bent down, picked him up, held him full Simba up to the fountain. The worst part is that poor Verne acted like this happened every day! He just said, "Thanks," and walked away.

Extra

I SHARE THIS story because there will be times in your life that you will have an opportunity to make a difference and you may not know what to do. Don't let the fear of maybe doing the *wrong* thing keep you from doing *some*thing. I am not encouraging intentional negligence, but if your heart is to genuinely care for others, it is rare that you will veer too far off from what is needed. Bottom line is sometimes you will look the fool, but if your heart is in the right place, you will just end up with a little more humility. Remember, no matter how bad you screwed up today, you didn't full Simba a man.

Scary Stories

B<small>EFORE</small> I <small>GRADUATED</small> from high school, I had almost died four times.

The first time I must have been about eleven years old. My mom had sent my sister Sara and I to stay with my grandparents for a month. As you know, I loved them and all of our family trips to their house. One morning my grandma told us she had a surprise set up: her friend Bob was going to take us white water rafting. I had seen people do this many times, since they lived right near the river that ran through town.

I was pretty excited; we had been on the jet boat, which was a local tourist destination, but had never been down the rapids. I had seen the excitement of white water rafting depicted in many soda commercials, and it looked great. It was just a little weird that my grandmother was going to let a man we didn't know take us away on his watercraft for about eight hours, but I don't have time to unpack that baggage right now.

We showed up expecting to meet a young man from her church with a raft and a bunch of gear. Instead we were greeted by a seventy-five-year-old man who had a wooden dingy. This boat was so small that a grown man couldn't lie down in it without his feet sticking out. Also it was the only piece of equipment the old guy had, other than some rope to tie it off and his lunch pail. None of this concerned my grandmother in any way.

It took about twenty minutes of floating through the rocky river before I was underwater. I popped up, quite confused as to what had happened, and saw my sister floating as well. The old man was on a rock with what was left of his boat upside down next to him. Bob threw the rope to us, and we were all able to make it to shore. We no longer had a boat or any supplies and this was long before cell phones existed. It took us a couple hours of walking through the woods and carefully crawling under an electric fence and through a pile of manure on the other side before we found someone who let us use their house phone. It was all terrifying and, to be honest also the coolest thing that had ever happened to me up to that point.

My second brush with death was a church group trip to the base of the Grand Canyon when I was sixteen. A monsoon appeared without warning and washed out all the trails leading back up. About four hours of carefully climbing out of the canyon with many close calls made me feel very lucky to have made it out alive. The third time was when my future brother-in-law took us off-roading and forgot to lock the hubs. I don't know much about off-roading, but we learned very quickly that locking the hubs was critical . . . as we carefully climbed out of a vehicle precariously teetering on the edge of a cliff.

The irony of all of these terrifying experiences is the

scariest story was also the least dangerous. When I was seventeen, my bandmates were also my best friends. If we weren't playing our own show on the weekend we were usually attending someone else's. Our drummer, who we called Munch, even though his name was Ryan, had asked us to go with him to see his uncle play at a little coffeehouse in Whittier. His uncle was a pretty interesting character. He was the last surviving hippie I knew of. He played a twelve-string acoustic guitar and covered everything from old protest songs to "Puff, the Magic Dragon."

We were at the coffee shop for a while listening to the other musicians and poets as we waited for Munch's uncle to do his thing. He told us he wouldn't be up for another hour and if we wanted to go grab some food and come back, we could. Munch had told us about a delicious burger place we were dying to try, so we walked from the coffeehouse to the burger place. Like many cities in Southern California, Whittier has parts that tend to be more walkable than others. This burger place was located in a higher crime area, but we didn't think twice about it.

When we left the burger place to walk back, though, the sun had gone down and there were hardly any streetlights on this road—which made it very dark. As we were walking, we saw a van with its windows covered and headlights turned off driving toward us. We all got quiet. The sketchy van passed us, and we felt a sense of relief. A few seconds later we heard a screech as the van made a very sharp U-turn and started heading our direction again. This is when everything went into slow motion. Out of the corner of my eye I saw the van door slide open and a hand emerge with a gun.

We took off full speed running. I am not a runner by any means, but in that moment I could have won a gold medal. I had made it a few blocks in what seemed like no time. We heard a loud pop and looked back to see Munch falling to the ground as he grabbed his calf, screaming. The rest of us immediately hit the ground, face-planting hard on the sidewalk. The van pulled up to us, and I just knew we were goners. Then nothing happened. For about twenty seconds I waited for the inevitable before looking up to see a guy about my age pointing a squirt gun at me. He soaked our shocked faces, laughed and then sped off.

It turns out that they had somehow attached a water-balloon launcher to the van door and shot Munch at close range. He saw the "gun" in the guy's hand and heard a loud pop as his leg felt terrible pain. He felt his wet pant leg and really thought he had been shot. In the moment *this was not funny*. It was definitely not a cool thing for those guys to do, but in hindsight I'm sure they found it somewhat hilarious.

Extra

OUR IMAGINATIONS HAD painted a picture that the worst scenario was happening, and even though reality was much different, at the time it felt so real. Whenever I get into dark moments of the soul and let my imagination take me down a path I don't want to be on, I remind myself of the time I was convinced a drive-by was happening. My other stories were very near death, and although I was not in any real danger that night in Whittier, I had tricked myself into thinking it was the end.

I wish I could say that was the last time I felt hopeless, but even to this day there are mornings when I struggle to find a silver lining. After all, we're only human. There will always be new giants that make us question our future. But listen, it is actually possible to be aware of the challenges you are currently facing without being paralyzed by them. Deal with the reality, but realize it is only temporary and does not need to be a defining factor in your life. That small shift will help you find the extra that you need to get past an uncomfortable ordinary.

Let's Make a Movie!

LONG BEFORE SHARING silly videos was a thing everyone appreciated, before we ever had YouTube, my friends and I had the VHS. The VHS was a tape that had been passed around from person to person, shared at parties, and copied a hundred times over. It was nothing more than a collection of random videos we made to try to get each other to laugh.

I remember the first time I got asked to be a part of one of these videos. A guy a few years older than me—who would for a short time become the youth pastor at the church I attended before becoming a stand-up comedian and bartender—called me one day. He said, "Your sister tells me you have a video camera. I'm coming to pick you up and we are gonna make a movie." This was one of the weirdest phone calls and the coolest invitations I had received. From the time I was five years old I knew I wanted to make movies. So when he used that phrase I was in immediately.

He and his buddy picked me up and I hopped into the back seat of his Chevy Chevelle that we all referred to as La Bamba. I asked what the movie was going to be about and he said, "Just start filming. You'll get the idea and we are gonna improvise." I hit record and the two guys in the front seat began telling the story about how earlier that day Christian Slater had been arrested, and we were on our way to find him to get the real story.

It was both ludicrous and fantastic. I had always thought that to make something you needed a plan. I found the permission to just make something—for no other reason than to make it—freeing. These videos just became silly things we did for fun and to share with others. We made videos about anything that inspired us, with very little thought as to what the end product would look like. One video was about an oversized curb in the neighborhood. It was about a foot higher than it needed to be, and we made a sketch about a kid who tried to jump over the biggest curb and didn't make it. Another one was about trying to drink water from one of those water jug refill machines outside of the grocery store. We even made an entire series about a Christmas tree that came to life when no one was looking.

Recently I came across one version of the VHS and laughed with my kids at the absurdity we had created. We did these videos with no script, no budget, and very little equipment. None of us had a computer that we could edit on, so we made up our own way to edit. We had two VCRs plugged into each other, and had to coordinate hitting *play* and *pause* simultaneously to make edits. If we wanted to add music, someone else would quickly unplug the audio cable and patch in a CD player to add the sound. The idea of completion overrode any desire for perfection.

Making these sketch videos brought us so much joy.

There was no ad revenue, and no one was trying to add to their portfolio. We made the things simply to make them. I have always tried to keep one thing going that serves this creative purpose. As a creative individual you can't always be making things just for money. Some things need to be made just so those ideas can exist outside of your head.

Extra

I AM SO grateful for that season of low-pressure creativity. Often in an effort to create something extraordinary, we can put so much pressure on ourselves and on the project. Never forget that there was a time when we did things not out of obligation or because they provided financial rewards, but simply for the joy of creating itself. We gave ourselves a wonderful gift—*permission*.

I believe that all of us need a creative outlet. Regardless whether your livelihood is made in the arts, we can all benefit from the joy of creating things. Whether it is woodworking, gardening, crafting, painting, or cooking. Give yourself a creative task and the space to fail miserably at it. The lower the stakes the better. There is always time for refinement and growth, but if you put too much pressure on yourself you will never create anything. Don't allow the fear of failure to keep you from making a move. You will be bad at it the first time. Just choose an outlet, lower the bar, and hit the accelerator.

Ice Cream Man

APRIL 17, 2020: Today I feel like shit.

I am forcing myself to sit down and write, to work, to accomplish anything at all on what feels like a terrible day. As I write these words we are in the middle of a global pandemic due to the COVID-19 coronavirus. Everyone is quarantined in their respective houses wondering what is next. As a live event performer, I will be quite honest: I am terrified. Up to this point, my family's livelihood as well as my personal identity has been wrapped up in traveling the country performing for large groups of people. If you are reading this in the future, perhaps my concern will be warranted or perhaps it will be laughable.

Currently, I don't know what normal will look like after this. Six weeks ago I was a successful performer on the cusp of what I thought was a major breakthrough in an industry that now seems nonexistent. I am certain entertainment will exist in the future, but I am not sure what form it will take and if I can have a place in it. I don't write any of this to, say, depress you or make you feel sorry for me. I am just realizing, once again, that wonder is incredibly important. It allows us to get outside of our current situations and realities and travel to somewhere altogether different.

Wonder is more than a luxury, it is critical for surviv-al.

Wonder is all around us, and it takes shape in many forms. Today, wonder entered my life through a Choco Taco. Yes, you heard me right: a frozen dessert modeled after a taco just transported me to another world. I was having my daily existential crisis, wondering what this is all about, when my kids asked if they could have ice cream. Since we are unable to leave the house right now due to quarantine, we've stocked up on all the essentials and a few special items like ice cream snacks to keep the kids from going to stir-crazy. When I told my wife I wanted a Choco Taco (for the last two years we have eaten very little dairy), Katie looked at me like I was crazy. Maybe it is her love for me, or perhaps she saw that spark of joy in my eyes and knew I needed some-thing to break me out of the moment I was stuck in. She made me a deal: I could have one if I went and wrote a chapter in the book about it.

I realize you may feel cheated now: I brought you down a rabbit hole telling this story, and the whole reason was so I could have ice cream. If you feel that way you are right. That is the only reason I dragged myself off the living room floor to write today . . . but there is more. Once I tried that ice cream, something shifted. I was instantly teleported back in time to when I was a kid and we would hear the ice cream man driving in our neigh-borhood. Since we lived by a park, there was always an ice cream truck making the rounds. There was more than one, in fact. One was super sketchy—a middle-aged white guy with a Bob Ross afro playing Kenny G over the loudspeaker. You heard that right. We always avoided this guy. Even as kids we just knew it wasn't a good idea, and remember—we'd all walked on hot coals.

The other truck, though, had that all-familiar "ice cream man" song playing. This song was like a dog whistle for kids. No matter what was happening, when we heard this song we were filled with joy, hope. and excitement. I remember hearing it faintly and leaping to my feet in order to beg mom or dad for cash before we missed it. When the truck pulled up, we began reading all the menu stickers on the side of the van to see what we would have. I don't know about you but the options seemed limitless when I was a kid. Our ice cream man had a menu that would put the Cheesecake Factory to shame. We would form a line, place our orders, and then enjoy the deliciousness that came from our parents trusting us to bring them any change left.

Extra

As I PLOPPED myself down on the edge of our porch eating my ice cream I realized that those times I was reminiscing about were also difficult. I guarantee you there were times that I sat eating ice cream while my grandfather was sick and later dying, or while my parents were talking about getting a divorce. Yet we found a moment of reprieve, of respite from the chaos surrounding us. In the midst of great sorrow, there also exist moments of extreme joy. I still am uncertain about the future, I am not sure what will become of the industry I love, but I also just had a great laugh with my family, and we were together, and I had ice cream.

In our house we have had to deal with some harsh realities. My daughters on one hand have had to grow up a little faster than I did. We all can stress and feel anxious about the future. There will be times for reflection, contemplation, and planning, but there also needs to be some time set aside for ice cream. Today as you wrestle with new challenges and discoveries, take a moment to a trigger a good memory. If you need an ice cream to help get you there—do it! Part of why remembering our childhood experiences is so important is because it reminds us that all along there is joy and pain, defeat and victory. There is something about remembering we have survived so much that tells us *we can survive this too*. Now put a bookmark here, stop what you're doing, and go get a yourself a frozen treat. Steve Martin had a bit in his act about how when you're playing banjo, it's really hard to feel sad or angry. I think that goes for Rocky Road too.

Cancel Your Plans but Still Go

A FEW YEARS ago Katie and I were in desperate need of a vacation. My brother and sister-in-law, who happen to be some of our best friends, felt the same way. We decided to do something different. We would take a week-long vacation and, apart from choosing a destination, we would not plan anything else before we got there.

Vacation is meant to be relaxing, but often in an effort to get the most out of our time we overplan. Time away becomes so packed with schedules and itineraries that you end up coming home exhausted instead of refreshed. I had been traveling so much that I had a surplus of frequent flyer miles. We decided we would use miles for the flight and hotel, but other than that, everything else would be spontaneous. New York was the destination and that is all we knew.

We landed and checked into our hotel. That evening, without knowing what to expect we journeyed into the city for one of the most magical nights. We happened upon an elevator that we took to the roof of a skyscraper and saw the most glorious 360-degree view of Manhattan. We had mouth-watering shawarma from a street cart and found a bakery whose banana pudding would put your grandma's recipe to shame. Each morning we walked out of our hotel and basically flipped a coin to pick a direction to walk and start exploring. We ate at amazing restaurants without ever using Yelp. We even took in a Broadway show without ordering tickets months in advance—and got last-minute, twenty-five–dollar center seats! What took place over that week was, hands down, the best trip any of us ever have had. Each night we went to bed excited that we had no idea at all what to expect the next day.

Extra

I HAVE OFTEN looked back on what made that trip so special. I think a big part of it was we removed the pressure of having to do all the things or make things perfect. Instead, we just were present and let each day unfold in front of us. Every night we went to bed satisfied and our expectations were never let down... because we went into it without any.

I like to call this experience a parachute vacation. No plans, just land and see what happens. I have begun to apply this approach to other life experiences. All too often we are so focused on the goal and destination, we miss the joy of the journey. Sometimes the best parts of anything are the unplanned interruptions. If we are so busy that we don't have time to take a break and see what is around the corner, we might miss out on a great adventure. If I find myself nervous about an upcoming event, or start to feel too much pressure to reach a certain outcome, I will decide to parachute instead.

Usually if you are anxious about something coming up, it is because you have built up expectations. You think if it doesn't turn out the way you imagined, it will be a failure. If we can learn to remove that pressure and just be fully engaged with our experiences, we will live with more joy. It is our desire to be in control that leads to disappointment when things happen differently than we would have liked them to. Never forget that some of the most extraordinary things were not what you originally had planned. So leave your expectations at home and pack your parachute instead.

Instant Affinity

A FEW YEARS back I heard comedian Martin Short coin a phrase that put words to a way I have approached relationships for many years. When meeting someone new, he said, he seeks to develop "instant affinity." If you are committed to developing extraordinary relationships, I can't think of a better approach to take than this.

We have all walked away from meeting a stranger and said something like, "I feel like I've known them my whole life." Perhaps you credited this to coincidence or the fact that you just had a lot in common with them. But what if you had the ability to create these type of connections all the time? To instantly engage with others and build lasting connections? That is what this chapter is all about.

Being a full-time magician and speaker for the last twenty years, I have had to learn how to quickly connect with others in both large and small group settings. Whether I am hosting my weekly *About to Break* podcast, meeting a client for coffee, or presenting a keynote for 2,500 conference attendees, my livelihood depends on immediate engagement. More importantly, though, the deep relationships I have been able to develop have been oxygen to my soul.

This ability is not about having to be an extrovert or being able to do card tricks. Connecting in this way will help you regardless of the position or situation you find yourself in. CEOs, teachers, stay-at-home parents, and entertainers all survive and thrive based on their ability to connect with others. Each of us will play many roles in our lifetime; if you apply this principle, the result will be a deeper level of connection in both your personal and professional lives.

It is important to realize this is an internal process. It is not about manipulating others or getting something out of them. It is about doing the work to be someone that others like to be around and want to work with. How you connect with strangers has a huge impact on the trajectory of your career and social life.

First impressions are overrated. Do you remember who told you, "You never get a second chance to make a first impression?" Possibly your mother on your way to meet your first real date or your high school guidance counselor explaining the job interview process. We have all heard this so often that the statement is easily dismissed or, worse, it becomes the focus of our interactions. I remember hearing this on orientation day at my first job working for Peanuts TV and Appliance. I was fifteen and my takeaway from the statement was, "Kid, act like someone better."

The challenge with trying to make a good impression is that it inevitably leads to our being disingenuous. We find ourselves saying what we think the other person wants to hear, acting in a way that is acceptable to the masses and losing sight of who we are in the process. There have been countless TV episodes about someone who, in an effort to make a good impression, created a new persona they then had to try and keep up. On television this is hilarious, but in life it is exhausting.

Instant affinity is not a switch we turn on when we need someone to like us. It is a new way of being. When we try to make a good impression, all of our attention is on our actions. Did I say the right thing? Wear the right outfit? Shake hands properly? Affinity supersedes these otherwise superficial actions. You could make a list of people you have met who have the proper look and all the right moves. Yet somehow you have no connection to them after meeting.

What if—rather than turning on the charm—you could learn to operate in a way that allowed you to consistently make deep connections? This approach is a shift from focusing on what you do to who you are being with other people. The opposite of focusing on making a good impressions is the statement, "Just be yourself." The problem with this direction is that there is no emphasis on the type of person you are being. If a person with narcissistic tendencies were to just go out and be themselves, the results would not be deep personal connections. The focus should be on adding value to other people, not reiterating how great we are.

Remember that experiencing the extraordinary in our relationships means taking a different approach than is often seen.

Many people change their persona based on who they

are with or where they are at. They wear different masks at home, at the office, at play, and online. A way that we often approach relationships is by thinking *What can this person do for me?* or *What can I get out of this connection?* It can be very helpful to make a list of your relationship needs, perfect client, etc. In the process of defining what you are looking for externally, I believe it is also helpful to take a deeper look internally. *Is who I am being adding value to others?* Much has been written on how to train others, but this approach is about going into training ourselves.

Michael, a comedian friend of mine, tells a story about walking out of a comedy club one night after being surrounded by people laughing and enjoying themselves. He looked across the street and saw a man sleeping on the sidewalk and it was clear that he had nothing to his name. Michael thought to himself, *How could I possibly make that man laugh?* and his answer was that it would be impossible. However, he could give him the opportunity to laugh. For Michael, this realization changed everything about how he is onstage and off. He no longer goes into a situation looking at what he can get from someone else, but instead looks for opportunities to give.

In full disclosure, instant affinity is not always easy for me. In a world that is very self-centered, it is easy for me to be so concerned about my task that I forget who I am being in the process. I am sad to say I have done this more times than I can count. However, I have also had countless times in which I chose to focus on affinity and have developed relationships with strangers than have become vital to my existence. Vance is one of those friends.

I met Vance at an event where he and I were both working. It should have been a one-time event and a one-time interaction. It is because of the choice Vance made to lean into connection that he and I are still so close today. Granted, we don't see each other every day. We don't even live in the same state. But when we do meet up, it is like no time has passed. This year alone we found ourselves eating at a food truck in a state neither of us are from, and on a recent tour I crashed at Vance and his wife Chelsea's place in Nashville. As Katie and I opened their Christmas card this year we smiled at the gift of friendship instant affinity gave us once again.

One of the most relationally and financially rewarding experiences in my life happened because I said yes to something most people would have said no to. In Los Angeles there are so many amazing variety shows that showcase talent and are a blast to perform at. From a financial perspective it makes no sense, though, because you don't get paid, have limited performance time, and can spend a small fortune in gas and parking just to get to the venue. I was asked to perform for a variety show in Santa Monica one night. I would spend three hours driving round trip to perform for five minutes on a show with other acts I had never heard of. I said yes—and it changed my life.

That night I met two other performers who would become great friends. My buddy Nick was one of them, and we talk or text almost every day. We have ridden the roller coaster of entertainment together and have also walked several miles just to get a donut; he's the best. Also that same evening there happened to be a booking agent from back east in the audience, who has not only become a wonderful friend but has also booked me for one of the single largest contracts ever. All because I said yes and chose to put connection over currency.

Extra

THERE WAS A time not that long ago that I would have said no to an opportunity like the one I just mentioned. I would have stayed home or possibly gone, done my five-minute set and left. I used to fear situations in which I would be required to meet new people. Often in these circumstances, I felt out of place and would regularly apologize for my awkwardness—or even for my presence. But my lovely wife Katie—my voice of reason—challenged me to focus on who I was being and to connect with people on a real, genuine level. That very difficult conversation we had one evening almost ten years ago started me on this journey of development, and I am so grateful that she challenged me in this way.

Whether you make your living behind a microphone, behind a desk, or in front of a chalkboard, I would encourage you to approach life focusing on how *who you are* affects the world and not the other way around. Meeting new people becomes so much more fun when you realize you are there to give them something not trying to get something from them. It is much easier to open the door for someone who is delivering flowers than for someone delivering a subpoena.

Does the thought of taking this approach excite you? Does it seem daunting or as if it is too late in the game to get started? The truth is, it is never too late to make a shift toward affinity. The type of connections we are looking to build are strong enough to overcome an awkward first encounter. You have the possibility to not only to make incredible connections in the future, but to redefine how you have been perceived in the past. The choice is yours to make and the benefits are yours to receive.

I fully believe you can find a common-ground connection to anyone who is willing to explore with you. Over half of the guests I have had on my podcast were perfect strangers prior to their appearance. However, I have built the podcast conversation using this idea of instant affinity and the result has been deep personal connections following the show. Katie often teases me that when I am going to meet a stranger to record, I will leave in two hours with a new best friend—and most of the time she is right! You can experience the same thing in your interactions if you choose to pursue genuine connection.

In short, instant affinity all comes down to being present and being real. This means full engagement, which can be challenging in the distracting world we live in. Every day we are bombarded with texts, emails, and phone calls. We look at social media posts and long to be somewhere different. People know when you are with them out of an obligation or if you are really present. They can also tell if you are being genuine or are putting up a front.

Take a moment and think about the last time you met someone new. Were you a hundred percent engaged or was your mind elsewhere? Were you actively listening or thinking about how you would respond once it was your turn to talk? If we are committed to experiencing that something extra in our encounters, then we need to bring a little extra to each meeting: focus on what we are giving and not what we are receiving. That is the key to powerfully connecting with others.

Houdini and the Inescapable Ego

WHEN I WAS a kid my fascination with Houdini was unrivaled. I had heard the legends, I read every book on his life. I even watched the movie with Tony Curtis that was great . . . except for when they said he died while performing his famous Water Torture Cell illusion. The truth is he died from a ruptured appendix when a young boxer punched him. The movie was so popular that many people think he really did die on stage—a misconception I'm certain Houdini would have loved.

What fascinates me most about Houdini is the fact that most of us since we were five knew that Houdini was a magician, that he was the best, and *none of us know why we know that*. The truth is, Houdini wasn't necessarily the most popular magician in his lifetime, but everything he did was about leaving a legacy. While his competitors like Thurston were busy filling theater seats, Houdini was more concerned with being remembered after his death. He went as far as leaving money in his will to hire a publicist to promote his death.

It is undeniable that Houdini met his goal and achieved the outcome he wanted. Still, the question is whether or not any of us should be taking this approach today. For Houdini it was all about the illusion of success and the image of being the greatest. Sadly, many people today live their lives that way, desiring fame for no reason and seeking an audience though they have no message to share.

The world of social media influencers is built upon this weird paradox—people who are famous for nothing other than being famous. Houdini would have crushed this game. Once a reporter asked Houdini what he thought about his competitor promising to make a horse vanish on stage that Saturday and Houdini, without knowing this or skipping a beat, said it was ridiculous and he would make an elephant vanish on Friday. All of this without knowing how to do it or where to find an elephant. Houdini pulled off the trick, which was reportedly pretty awful, but he understood only a few people would see the failed performance—but the whole world would see a news photo of him with the elephant.

Extra

WE CAN GO through life seeking pointless fame, or we can take the approach of putting beautiful things out into the world. Houdini's goal was a self-serving one. It fanned the flames of his ego and it made him known, but how much different would the world be if someone with that much influence had a message other than *I am the greatest*?

This is as much a challenge to myself as it is to anyone who might be reading. Show business is a tempting muse, and the bright lights of Hollywood are very attractive. Having sat in some of the biggest greenrooms in the industry, I can tell you that fame isn't all it's cracked up to be. I've sat with blockbuster stars and headliners who talk about how they wish they could just get back to the freedom of obscurity, to once again make something without the pressure of it having to be groundbreaking.

So here are a few questions that will allow you to check the vital signs of your intentions. Does your dream help build the dreams of others? What happens after you reach your goal? No matter what industry you are in, how will you use your influence? Are you doing what you can to make a difference with the influence you currently have? What do you want the message of your life to be? How are you sharing that message?

I can't speak for Houdini, but I often wonder if he were to have a conversation with his eight-year-old self, Erik Weisz, what would Erik say about how he turned out. You see, Houdini himself was an illusion. His persona was a combination of characteristics he picked up along the way. Even his name was taken from the great French illusionist Robert Houdin, who Houdini idolized until he eventually unmasked him with a tell-all book on how his tricks were done. Little Erik could have grown up to be whoever he wanted, and we have that same opportunity. We are all the scriptwriters of the stories they will tell about us. What is it that is holding you back from being the best version of yourself?

Houdini is undeniably the most recognized magician in history; he was highly innovative and copied by many.

He built a legendary persona, brick by brick, that captured the attention of generations still to be born. Yet I can't help but wonder what he could have done if his narcissism hadn't gotten in the way. He built something so gigantic that I suspect he started to believe his own hype. This man was able to escape medieval torture devices, straitjackets upside down in Times Square, and shackles while submerged in milk cans. The only thing he couldn't escape was his own ego.

Summer Camp Life

I LOVE SUMMER camp. I went as a kid, and for about thirteen years I served as a counselor helping to lead these camps. If I had to summarize what camp was in one word it would be *memorable*. Not only was the schedule always packed full of crazy fun, but there was always something unplanned that would become an unforgettable moment from then on. Having participated in over forty separate camp experiences, I have found some consistent themes that ensure camp feels more extra than ordinary.

I think expectation is a big part of why summer camp doesn't let people down. You go into it with the mindset that you will have an amazing experience and so you do. A lot can be said about approaching a moment saying, "I am here to make friends and I am here to make memories." I will say it again, having been to forty-plus camps, all of them have been their own version of awesome.

The power that perspective has on our experiences is huge. When I recall some of my favorite moments from camp trips, they sound like nightmares. Buses breaking down, 2:00 a.m. trips to the ER, and the camp speaker who disappeared are all light versions of what I am talking about. It seemed like at camp anything that could go wrong would, but our intention to have a great time overshadowed the reality of what we were experiencing.

Another thing that makes camp so great is, for the most part, everyone who goes to camp is fully present. We realize that this time is limited, and for a moment we stop thinking about the problems at home or the fight we had with someone before we left. At camp, everyone is all in. It is one of the few times I've seen people be able to shut off the outside world for a week or two. Because of this approach, you can develop deep relationships very quickly.

When I was going into high school, I went to a summer retreat our school held for incoming freshman. I didn't know a single person who was going to the school, but by the end of that week I was connected. I had friends who would be with me throughout high school, because the only agenda that week was relationship-building and memory-making. I remember all of the crazy games, skits, and activities—but mostly I remember the uninterrupted talks face-to-face without the interruption of TV and the Internet.

As a family we have experienced similar occurrences when we take camping trips together. When you are crammed in a minivan for two weeks driving around the country, you can't help but become stronger as a family. You will be forced to get along and forced to think of creative ways to have fun. A few years ago I was booked to perform magic at a series of summer camps in Texas. We took the most indirect way of getting there. We drove from Southern California to Yellowstone and camped for a week with my in-laws. The kids played in the woods with the cousins and had a blast. Then we drove down through Colorado to Texas, did the shows, and then drove home through New Mexico and Arizona. We put more than five thousand miles on our already tired van and made memories our kids will never forget.

I don't always approach life with a summer camp mentality, but when I do it is always better. I travel a lot as a full-time entertainer, and it isn't as glamorous as it seems. Before I hit the road, I used to think traveling for a living would be so awesome—and it is, but it also takes a toll on you. Most of my time is spent just trying to get to the next place. If I am booked in New York to perform for an hour, I will often take two full days just getting there and back. I guess I was technically in New York, but all I saw was a hotel, a rental car, and a ballroom.

So when I am traveling I am often quite exhausted. Sometimes I fight through this and approach travel as an opportunity for friendship and memory-making, although my temptation when I am at the airport is to put on my headphones, pull my hoodie over my head, and take a nap. Sometimes I don't ... and end up meeting someone like Henry. Henry was sitting next to me on a flight from LA to Phoenix. I never want to be the pushy guy on the plane who talks with someone who clearly needs a break, but something told me Henry wanted to chat.

Turns out he was on a trip to the East Coast to see his son, from whom he had been estranged for many years. A recent loss in the family had brought them back together and he was overjoyed to be reuniting with his child. When we exited the plane, we realized we both had long layovers, and I offered to buy Henry breakfast. We continued to chat about everything from movies, classic cars, and even mistakes we wish we could do over again. I never saw Henry after that, but we shared an amazing few hours together. I am so glad that on that particular day I didn't let how I was feeling keep me from being fully present.

Extra

RIGHT NOW AS I write to you, I have been overwhelmed with deadlines and to-do lists. My mind has been racing thinking about the news of the day and the implications it has for tomorrow. However, reminiscing about camp has made me realize that just being present in the moment you are in and with the people you are with can provide much-needed rejuvenation. I will make the choice, in the midst of my worry and responsibility, to treat today like it is summer camp. To not have today be a throwaway because dad was anxious. Instead I will finish my work, go inside the house, and figure out a way for our family to chase wonder tonight. I have found that pausing in the car before I enter the house and visualizing us all enjoying an evening together puts me in the right frame of mind. It's incredible how much this little practice can change the energy with which I enter the room.

It Happens

LET'S BE HONEST: sometimes life is pretty terrible. Sometimes bad things happen and there is no bright side, but usually when something awful happens it makes the best story. When you are at a dinner party or hanging till the wee hours of the morning with friends, you don't tell the stories about when everything went according to plan. You tell the stories about when all hell broke loose and the shit hit the fan. Frankly, your best material is about when it all went wrong. Learning to laugh about these terrible moments and embrace the beauty of those mistakes is all part of the process of life.

We live by many sayings in our house but one of my favorites is, "If it's going to be funny later, it should be funny now." If we will tell this story with joy for years to come, let's just start laughing together about it now. I know this is easier said than done, but I have lived through these moments both ways, and for me, finding the humor in our humanity brings us together. It is the great equalizer. We all make mistakes and we all deal with terrible situations. I guess if I am going to keep talking about this subject I should share a personal example.

Before I gave up my day job and became a full-time

entertainer, I was overseeing a team of six people and each of them had two interns. At the end of their internship we wanted to do something to appreciate them for their hard work. Naturally, I chose an evening at the Magic Castle, my home club and one of Hollywood's most elite establishments. So elite that even as a member, I couldn't get a dinner reservation on a busy Saturday. No problem, we would simply eat at another local spot and then head to the Castle for an evening of entertainment.

We decided to carpool with a coworker because they'd just gotten a beautiful, brand-new car. He and his wife were in the front seat, Katie and I were in the back. The rest of the team took a fifteen-passenger van as we made the trek into Hollywood. The restaurant the interns chose was a well-known Thai place and it was delicious. We ordered everything and I ate more than my share, but this is when I was younger and could do so with no problem. Remember being able to eat whatever you want and then follow the meal with any activity? "You guys want to head to the trampoline park?" "Sure, let's do this!"

We finished dinner and decided to go grab a coffee at Starbucks on the way to the Castle. Katie hadn't been feeling so well, so I decided to wait with her in the car with her while the team ran inside to get drinks. After about twenty minutes, I thought, *This is taking a while, we need to start heading to the show.* I told Katie that I would just run in and check on things. I stepped out of the car and started to head inside . . . and then it happened.

I should mention that at this point I felt fantastic. Not sick, not nauseous, no indigestion, but without a warning I had this powerful sensation that I should already be in the restroom. I started to say to Katie, "I think I need to—" That was all I could get out before everything came out. Without any effort or warning, I had just completely evacuated. My brand-new suit that I had just picked up from the tailor that afternoon was now the scene of a crime. Katie looked at me and said, "You didn't just . . ." and I replied, "Yeah, I did!"

I am still amazed at the level of poise I possessed as I carefully walked across the parking lot into the Starbucks. The place was packed. I kept my back along the wall and approached the bathroom like a ninja in a three-piece suit. Imagine my shock when I had to then walk all the way back to the front to get the door code. Eventually I made it in and did what I had to do. I was able to get them into the Castle while I headed home. The interns enjoyed their evening at the Castle and a lot of laughs were had at my expense. Oh yeah, my coworker still had to drive us back in his new car!

That evening I decided it was better to hang my suit up in the cab of my truck than to leave it in the house. Early the next day I got up to take the suit to the cleaners on my way to work, and someone had broken into the car and stolen the poop suit! I immediately starting roaring with laughter. The insanity of the last eighteen hours was just so much that all I could do was laugh. It was a terrible night, a huge embarrassment, a big financial expense, and I wouldn't change a thing.

Recently we took a once-in-a-lifetime trip. Simply by referring to it as *once in a lifetime* we were setting ourselves up for failure. There is no room for pressure in adventure. Nevertheless, my in-laws, who have traveled to many amazing and exotic places, had never been to the UK. Likewise, Katie and I had always wanted to make a trip to Ireland, Scotland, and England. So with my brother and sister-in-law as well as Katie's folks, we made plans to go last June.

It was one of the best trips we ever took. It was also full of chaos and calamity, but then again, that is how all the great adventures start. When we booked the trip to Ireland we parachuted in, making no plans other than the flights and where we would be staying. We found this lovely Airbnb that was across from a pub. The pub owned the rental and they were some of the most delightful people you could ever meet. We spent hours seated at the bar, having perfectly poured pints of Guinness. I could have spent the whole vacation in this little pub and been happy. Nevertheless, we decided to rent a car and drive the three-hour trip to the other side of the country to see the legendary cliffs.

If you have never been to Ireland, you should know the highways are not like the freeways in the states. You will meander through farmlands and back roads the whole journey, and it is a gorgeous countryside. About an hour into our road trip the rental car lost all power and would no longer accelerate. This is not what you want to have happen when you are trying to do a six-hour round trip in a day. We found out from the car company that it would be at least two hours before we could get a replacement vehicle, and we were pretty upset. Rather than stay in the service station parking lot complaining, we decided to take a walk and find our next adventure. We passed a wonderful park and a historic church. The groundskeeper just happened to be there and let us in for a tour. Then we walked one block further and came upon a castle! A glorious, nine hundred-year-old castle. The lower half of the castle had been turned into a restaurant and we had a great snack and a few more pints.

Before we left I thought, *What is the harm in asking for a tour?* I asked one of the wait staff and she said, "Well, we don't really give tours, but OK." We then proceeded to take the most amazing unofficial tour of this castle. Creaky ladders, undisturbed hallways and bedrooms that were still fully furnished. I felt like Indiana Jones looking for lost treasure. We had free rein of a castle that had been left mostly untouched for hundreds of years and we would have driven right past it if the car hadn't broken down. How lucky were we to have car trouble that day? When we reminisce about that fifteen-day trip, this two-hour interruption is everyone's favorite moment, hands down.

Extra

WE ARE WHO we are not only because of the good times, but also because of the challenges. One terrible night made it a lot easier to shake off small embarrassments that would have debilitated me before. In a way, pooping in my suit was a gift, just as car trouble in Ireland was. I encourage you to reexamine stories of embarrassment or weakness through the eyes of wonder. How can you reframe or retell that story so that it supports you moving forward? It's like when you see a movie you didn't like as a kid, but now, through a different lens you enjoy it so much more. Stories are powerful; they can build up or tear down. Make sure you seek a positive perspective on your experiences—even if every once in a while you poop your pants or get stuck on the side of the road in a foreign country where you barely understand the language. I don't know what lies ahead for you today, but just remember when trouble happens ... adventure might be knocking on your door.

The Kids Table

THERE IS A phenomenon that takes place at every family gathering and in nearly every family, and yet it often goes undiscussed. I am talking about the kids table. As early as I can remember when our extended family came together there would be a small card table or coffee table with a sheet over it. This would be designated as the kids table. I think the parents hoped we would not bother them long enough for them to talk about politics and the latest episode of *Thirtysomething*, a TV show that confuses me to this day.

The big secret that none of the kids would admit to each other is that we actually love the kids table. If you were lucky enough to be sitting at that wobbly folding table, there were no rules to be followed, no subjects that were off-limits; you could even be playing with your favorite toy while eating. What could be better? The kids table was a place of designated acceptance for all things that kids loved. You were welcome, flaws and all, at the kids table.

When you were at the kids table, it meant that you got to eat first. While the adults waited their turns, the parents would assemble our plates with the items they knew we would eat. You always got a bigger helping during these gatherings because the longer you ate, the more peace and quiet the parents could enjoy. When you are a grown-up, you have to wait your turn. Usually you end up stuck behind your aunt as she slows the line to ask if the Jell-O salad has gluten in it.

The most important thing you learn when banished to the kids table is that most adults are boring. Ever since I discovered this fact I have made it my personal mission to never be boring. Often this attitude gets me into trouble, because I let my inner child shine in the wrong environments. I get very uncomfortable when I feel like other adults are stuck in a boring situation. Out of courtesy I will try to remedy this and inevitably make a huge mistake.

A few months before I resigned my role at the church I took the youth and children's staff to a leadership seminar in Pasadena at a very prestigious school. Everything about this environment was stuffy, which was ironic seeing as we were there to talk about how to better connect with young people. We had met a few other people who were there from around the country. One table seemed to have a pretty good sense of humor so after lunch as I sat enjoying the last of my boba milk tea, I had an idea.

Boba are large balls of tapioca that are used in delicious tea drinks. I had previously discovered what I thought to be a revolutionary property of the boba ball. Because it was just smaller than the wide straw it was served with, you could launch them like a blow-dart gun. My current record was seventy-two feet. I was also really accurate, so I figured I could hit the large table sign in the center of the fun loving groups table about twenty feet away. On a whim I blew as hard as I could trying to hit the sign—but miscalculated and hit their pastor right in his eye. It was so fast that no one saw what happened; the whole room just saw him grab his eye and scream out expletives in pain.

I say this to bring up the fact that while I aged out of the kids table I still feel I belong there. You can take the guy out of the kids table but you can't take the kids table out of the guy. While on that particular day my desire for fun led me astray, more often than not I would say the experience of others is elevated when I treat all life like the kids table. Ironically, part of this meeting was about how kids need to spend more quality time with their family and the idea of separating them at another table isn't so helpful.

I agree to an extent. It isn't just enough, though, to bring children to the adult table. We need to maintain a bit of that childlike wonder and bring it into all adulthood. What if the adult table was as inclusive, encouraging, and fun as the kids table? What if we lived in a way that let everyone know they belong—that there is a place at the table for each of us? What if our table conversations weren't just based on what was going wrong in the world, but were filled with the hope and possibilities we felt all those years ago huddled around that card table? All of us will eventually get older, but if we're not in a hurry to grow up, the more likely we are to see the extraordinary when it makes its appearance.

Harry in Hollywood

I OFTEN JOKE with my family that we are *Hollywood adjacent*. I am not a famous entertainer, but I know a lot of people who are. It is quite hilarious how often my children will be watching TV or discussing a movie and Katie will say, "Wasn't that actor on your podcast?" or "Didn't you host a show with them?" It is a bizarre version of the six degrees of separation game we enjoy playing at home. I don't bring this up to boast about my mild entertainment success, I do it to explain the difference between *show business* and *stardom*. Someone who spent the first part of his life learning this was my wife's grandfather, Harry Watson.

Harry's start in the business was not intentional, it was geographical. His parents made their home in the area of Los Angeles we now call Echo Park right about the time that famed director Mack Sennett built his movie studio in the lot next to their home. This was the early days of Hollywood, and the movie industry was booming. Harry's father, Coy, got a job working in the pictures as a wire man: he was involved in making the flying carpets fly in the movie *The Thief of Bagdad*. Once the studio found out he had nine children, they realized they had access to an on-demand talent pool of children for the movies they were producing. Every day the kids would line up along the fence and the producers would say, "OK, we need three boys and a girl." Coy would hand the kids over the fence, and they would go off to work in the movies for the day. It became the new family business.

Harry and his siblings can be seen in films like *Mister Smith Goes to Washington* with Jimmy Stewart. Harry rode Shirley Temple on the handlebars of his bike in *Little Miss Broadway* and even played W. C. Fields's son in the movie *Barbershop*. Yet the most extraordinary thing about Harry was while he spent a ton of time in show business, the most joy he received was simply making his family smile.

One of my first encounters with Harry was at his brother's funeral. This was one of those times early in the dating relationship: you are close enough to the person you are dating to accompany them to a funeral, but it is still one of the only times you have been around their extended family. I was nervous, mostly because I tend to think funerals are hilarious. I know that sounds terrible— we are celebrating the life of someone we lost—but the whole setup gives me the giggles.

Needless to say, I was quite relieved when I saw the way Harry was handling the whole situation. He went over to one of the many flower arrangements that had been sent and removed a single rose. He broke off the stem but held the flower together, making it look like it was still whole. Then he would put on his most somber face, walk up to a guest and say, "My brother would have wanted you to have this." He would then offer them a flower and when they grabbed the stem he would walk away. The person would eventually look down and realize they were only holding the stem. Harry could be heard in the distance, giggling to himself.

For the few years I knew Harry before his passing, I felt a very kindred connection to him. Without explanation, we just got each other. We were show business people, and the best shows Harry did happened when no one was expecting it. When the grandkids had a birthday, he would bake silver dollars into the cake. This is dangerous, unsanitary, and something I will definitely do when my grandkids arrive. One of the best stories about Harry was whenever Katie and her cousins would come over to swim, Harry would put on his finest three-piece suit and go hang out by the edge of the pool—and act surprised when they threw him in. He did this every time.

Extra

HARRY TAUGHT ME that if you want to have a little extra in your ordinary, you need to save some extra for yourself. Let me explain.

There is a transaction that takes place as a performer. Whenever you go on stage you are giving energy and, hopefully, receiving energy. Moreover, sometimes you are having to give your audience the experience of emotions you might be struggling to have at that time, be it hope, joy, or whatever. So a challenge every performer faces is you can create an emotional deficit if you give all of this away without recharging.

A few years ago I was talking with my therapist about the toll several rough shows had taken on me. I don't agree that there are good audiences and bad audiences; however, there are audiences with varying degrees of energy. When you expend energy and don't get it back, it feels terrible. My therapist challenged me to always save some of the joy for myself and not to give everything away.

For me in practice that means I come up with jokes I never tell; I write them down in the notepad on my phone and occasionally read them to myself. We also have inside jokes and experiences as a family that I don't share on stage. It is important that you always keep a little bit of the magic and humor as a personal gift to yourself and those you love. When I am tempted to give too much away, I think of that scene in the *Goonies* where Mouth is in the wishing well. He holds up a coin, saying something like, "This one right here, this is my wish, my dream, so I am taking it back!" Sometimes we need to take back our dreams and save a little extra joy just for us.

How Not to Eat School Lunches

I HATE BOLOGNA. When you're a kid you have an eclectic palate. You will eat things that you would and never could eat as an adult. I remember watching the host of a popular children's TV show wrap a Kraft cheese single around a chocolate bar; I tried this and loved it. Today I would never do such a thing—but if you wrap a piece of cheddar cheese around an Oreo cookie, it's surprisingly delicious. I would try anything at least once but there was one thing I hated and that was bologna.

My sister Sara loved the stuff. She ate sandwiches that consisted of bologna, lettuce, and ketchup. She simply adored it. I don't know what it was that turned me off. Maybe it was the fact that no one knows what it is made of, or that it comes in a weird container I'd never seen anywhere else. Perhaps it was the terrible smell that wafted into your nostrils when that bizarre package opened with a pop.

As a kid, I never thought to ask for special stuff in my lunch. My mom was pretty great about mixing it up. All day at school I waited with anticipation for lunchtime, when I would open up my lunch pail the way YouTubers now open mystery boxes. My friend Ben never had this experience. He was from Montana, the tallest kid in the first grade, and he had soup every day. His mom would give him one of those giant green thermoses that construction workers drink coffee out of. It would be full to the brim with enough soup to feed an entire army.

One day we were sitting at the picnic tables, and I opened my lunch to find a bologna sandwich. Ben knew I hated bologna because when you are first-grade friends, you have no secrets. Seeing the disappointed look on my face as I unwrapped the foil wrapper, Ben leapt into action. In a single motion he pulled out the slice of bologna and threw it like a frisbee over the school fence. There was a house next door with a swimming pool, and Ben landed the lunchmeat right in center of their swimming pool. Every kid in the lunch area cheered. The next day everyone showed up with a bologna sandwich, and Ben led them all in a game of cold-cut Frisbee golf. The poor neighbor came out to see his pool covered in lily pads of bologna. He was furious and began to hurl them back at us with the pool skimmer. Having it rain wet slices of bologna is one of my greatest childhood memories.

A few weeks later I once again found myself the recipient of the world's worst sandwich. I was complaining to Ben when this kid Mark said he loved bologna but today he got a roast beef sandwich. This is when I learned about one of the greatest unspoken agreements of the playground: the swap. Mark offered to trade his sandwich for mine, straight up! I couldn't believe it. Both of us were given something we didn't want and yet ended up with exactly what we wished for.

I doubt there is anyone who ever attended elementary school who didn't swap their lunch at one point or another. Having spent a lot of time with my dad at swap meets, I saw adults doing the same thing. The very name *swap meet* comes from the fact that collectors would meet up to trade items they didn't want for ones they did. This can be a very useful tool on the journey of living an extraordinary life. My buddy Bob refers to this as using what you have to get what you want.

You may not have the financial or relational resources needed to break into your desired field. However, all of us have something at our disposal that we can use to get what we want. How can you use something you have to do something you have always wanted to do? When I decided to make my first TV special, I knew I would have to operate this way. I bartered and traded services with lots of friends to be able to pull off the experience. One of my favorite parts of the special has a very strange backstory.

Ever since I first saw the vintage footlights that illuminated the stage at classic theaters, I knew if I ever did my own show, I had to have some. Once we planned a date to film and booked my favorite theater as a venue, I started looking to acquire footlights. I immediately found out that not only are they rare, but they are ridiculously expensive. Most were made out of solid brass and had a cool sea shell design. So I started thinking, *What can I use to get the look I want?* Then one day I was looking at a Halloween costume catalogue and saw the solution: mermaid bras. That's right! Those plastic mermaid bras they sell during the Halloween season were perfect. I bought a bunch of them, along with a string of Christmas lights. I painted them gold and mounted them in front of the lights on some black boards. The team at the theater loved them so much that I donated them. So if you ever see a famous comedian who taped a special at one of the premier theaters in Los Angeles, they are performing behind footlights I made out of mermaid bras.

Extra

WHAT IS AN area that you feel like you have been hitting a wall? Perhaps you have been waiting to have more time, more money, or more resources before pursuing that goal. Take a moment to shift your focus from what you don't have to what you *do* have. How can you use what you have to get what you want? No more waiting, my friend, because time is short. Go out there and think about creative substitutions or trades that will morph your ordinary into something extraordinary.

Take a Walk!

I HAVE ALWAYS hated exercise. In school, PE was never something I looked forward to. In addition to having to run laps in the middle of a hot day, the fact that I had to change clothes in front of all the guys in my class was complete torture for a husky kid. Still, this didn't stop me from attempting to find a sport I could connect with. I tried baseball, basketball, and even played an entire season of high school football. To this day I do not know all the rules to that game.

As an adult I tried tennis, and even golf one time. I am so naturally terrible that I could spend a small fortune becoming mediocre at golf. All that said, for years people said, "Why don't you just go for walks?" Walks? What good would that do? The truth is, it does a ton of good. Not only does walking burn calories and get your heart going, it has done wonders for my mental health. You see, I have always been the carefree guy, the happy-go-lucky, no worries or concerns guy.

And then the first panic attack happened.

Anxiety is a strange visitor who shows up unannounced. What puzzles me is I have walked with my wife through her challenges with anxiety for years and didn't see it sneaking up on me as well. People rarely talk about what panic attacks look or feel like, but they do talk about what heart attacks look and feel like. This is why when I had my first full-blown panic attack, I thought I was going into cardiac arrest. Worst of all, it happened right before a show at my favorite venue in the world—the Magic Castle.

My buddy James and I were performing a show we wrote specifically for the Castle. It was our second night and the first three shows had gone amazingly. We even got some pretty high praise from the entertainment director, and I was feeling great. However, just before they loaded the audience in for the first show of the evening, I started to feel a little flushed. This then turned into a sensation I have only ever felt when riding on a roller coaster. You know that feeling when your gut goes into your chest and you feel weightless? It was like that. Then my hands and feet went cold. I was certain it was a heart attack. After a trip to Cedars Sinai and a barrage of tests, the doctor asked me, "Do you ever deal with stress?"

Friends, I have been in the entertainment business long enough to know that the stress of uncertainty doesn't go away. We are in a strange business: in one week you might make more than enough to carry you through a few months, but then have no work come in the next few months. Anyone in show business can tell you there is no certainty in this industry. For some it leads to panic attacks; others become workaholics for fear of the future. Jay Leno famously never spent the money he made as the host of the *Tonight Show*. Instead he lived off doing stand-up gigs five or six nights a week—and this man has more than you would need in several lifetimes.

Once I realized that the months of stress I was feeling had started to manifest in physical symptoms, I decided I needed some physical activity as an outlet. I began taking walks around the neighborhood. These walks helped me process my thoughts in a way that was empowering. I now walk most days, and if I don't, everyone knows the difference. I usually walk at least five to six miles. Along the way I mull over whatever is on my mind; it is a wonderful way to start the day.

As I have been writing this book and reexamining moments from my youth, I have struggled the last few days to come up with stories I haven't already shared. I have been a bit frustrated and did not want to walk this morning. I still got up and went out . . . and my mind was flooded with memories of growing up. Things I began to see on the walk triggered wonderful and silly memories of my childhood. My writer's block was instantly cured, not by starring at a computer screen and saying to myself, "Think! Think!" No, I got out of my rut by getting out of bed and walking among the trees.

I have found these walks are more than a physical activity, they are a spiritual one. They help put me in the right frame of mind at the start of the day. I have never been disappointed at the end of a long walk; but I have felt the negative side effects of not doing it when I knew I should. Having these kind of habits are critical for the creative process. We need to have rituals that are good for us, nonnegotiable times to reflect and recharge our emotional batteries.

Extra

IT'S EASY TO recognize the importance of self-care; it is another to actually make the time for it. Especially if you are intentional about caring for others. As a parent it is really easy to neglect time for yourself or with your spouse for the sake of the kids. We say things like, *They just need me right now* and *It's OK, I am sacrificing for them.* I know this all too well. For years when I worked as a pastor at a church, I would regularly find myself in a terrible place because I had neglected self-care. Worse, I often neglected my family's needs because I was so focused on the ministry or task at hand.

I have found that the longer I go without caring for my emotional, physical, and spiritual health, the more I am rolling the dice on everything breaking down. After that first panic attack it became a regular occurrence. For nearly three weeks I couldn't leave my house without having the symptoms return. In fact, I began to question if I would ever feel normal again. Up until that point I had been trying to book shows, carving out an income to provide for my family. After the panic attack, though, I realized that if I don't protect my personal health, I won't have anything to offer others.

I am a pretty driven person. I have a strong work ethic and can push through a lot. Dealing with anxiety doesn't mean that you aren't strong or that you can't handle the pressure. The reality is sometimes our circumstances are too much to carry alone. At some point we all will come to the end of ourselves. We will see the true limitations of our feeble humanity—and that is a great place to be. The more we understand our weaknesses, the better equipped we are when struggles show up.

About to Break

LAUNCHING INTO A profession as a full-time performer after a thirteen-year career detour was not easy. I had finally decided to do the one thing I had known I was supposed to do since I was seven. I had been married for eleven years and we had two little girls. I was past the point of settling down, but I had found myself forced to pursue another avenue to pay the bills. After six jobless weeks, I talked to Katie and said if I don't at least try my hand at full-time entertainment I will regret it—and she was on board 100 percent. We agreed to give it a go, knowing that if it didn't work, I would take an office job or work at Starbucks to keep us afloat.

The first thing I did was to reach out to friends who might have connections and could help me find some work. You see, I had given up performing completely as part of the process I went through trying to figure out if we should stay at the church we were attending. Until that point I'd been performing about seventy shows a year that not only brought me joy but subsidized the low pay I received as a youth pastor. I was struggling with knowing which way to go and magic was a huge escape for me. But I knew that I needed to step away from it to be able to see the church situation more clearly, so I quit performing cold turkey. I took down my website, changed my phone number, and sold all my props. Less than a year later, I had left the church and decided to go full-time into entertainment.

All that to say, when I started performing as my sole source of income just eight years ago, I was starting over from scratch. Luckily some of my friends came through with show opportunities, and some even lent me the props I needed until I could afford to replace mine. Those first few years were a roller coaster. Pursuing full-time entertainment is a daunting task if you are young and single. As a dad and a husband, the weight I felt was heavy. At the same time, the joy I felt from doing the thing I love most was a new experience for me.

This life is always a mix of up and downs. Some months you make no money and then the next month you may make the most money you've ever seen. It took lots of therapy and still takes lots of meditation and long walks to be able to live with the lack of balance. There was a time about three years in when I was feeling very down and discouraged. I was telling myself I started too late and would never make this into a career. Then I started hanging out in comedy club greenrooms and hearing other performers talk about their highs and lows between sets. I realized in those conversations that it wasn't me . . . it was the business.

I began my weekly podcast as a reason to justify having more of these conversations. It started as a passion project and something to focus my energy on when I wasn't working as much as I wanted to. I decided to call the show *About to Break*—because in this business, all of us are either close to a big career breakthrough or a mental breakdown. I interviewed over 150 creative individuals who have made their living as actors, musicians, jugglers, directors, artists, and more. While the experiences and backgrounds vary from guest to guest, the theme of trying to do what you love and pay the bills is present in every conversation.

These amazing people are doing their best to break into an industry before it breaks them. Perhaps you can relate. Have you felt the pull of not wanting to just work to make a living and yet often having to compromise the best for the immediate? You may have even felt the pressure to "get a real job" or "grow up and stop dreaming." Those phrases don't even have to be vocalized to be felt. It all stems from what our idea of success is.

How do you define success? What does an abundant life look like to you? When I was a kid I picked up on the message our culture was putting out about success very early on. I think most people who are drawn to the creative arts notice the narrative quicker because it is contrary to the things we are most passionate about. At school the big takeaway early on was that the goal is to get a good job. That phrase—*good job*—was never explained, but you find out eventually that a good job equates to a nice salary, benefits, and stability.

Now if this is what drives you, don't let me discourage you—but if you are one of the dreamers who would rather fulfill a purpose than a position, I have some thoughts to share with you. Our modern educational system was formed around the American Industrial Revolution and the need for a massive workforce who understood math and science. Since those subjects were critical for workers of the day, we built an educational hierarchy that prioritized those subjects ahead of more creative endeavors.

The reward for getting a good education was you would be qualified for a good job and be set for life. But the challenge we are currently facing is our school system is still set up for this—but we can no longer keep the promise. Students are graduating with multiple degrees, massive student loan debt, and are not able to find a good job. Meanwhile there has been a massive boom in the gig economy, in which fourteen-year-olds with an iPhone and a YouTube account are building massive followings and making insane amounts of money in advertising revenue. Yet so many people still believe that the old model is to just get a degree and take whatever job will have you.

My quest to be a full-time performer may sound very romantic, and you might be all fired up to quit your job to pursue your dream—which maybe you should do— but first let me clarify a few things. I am not saying that getting a college degree isn't a valuable experience. I took six years to get a two-year degree and then took ten years off before going back to school and finishing my bachelor's degree, because it was something I always wanted to do. However, having a degree is not the guaranteed ticket it once was. We need to be careful to not perpetuate this out-of-date idea to young people.

I am incredibly grateful for parents who never once made me feel anything but proud of my creative endeavors. My mother was never too busy to pick a card so I could practice my magic. She would drive me an hour from our house so I could attend a magic club and then sit in the car while I spent hours learning the newest tricks. All the while, my parents never put pressure on me to monetize my skills too early or become a star at an early age. Whenever my sister or I showed a spark of interest in a subject, they would use the limited funds they had to pour fuel on our passion. Maybe that wasn't your experience, but I am here now telling you that you are not alone, and it is *never* too late to make a move.

Pursuing your dreams is hard! That is why most people never finish their book, launch that business, or create a product they know could make a huge difference. If you take the route to be a creative entrepreneur, you'd better be ready to work. It may be years before you can make your full living doing it. Don't let the fact that you have to have a day job or a side hustle get you down. Working to support yourself and your family is a noble thing.

The idea that entertainers or entrepreneurs have an easy life is not an accurate description of reality. I remember finding out that a friend got paid thirty thousand dollars for being in a national car commercial. Most people would feel that was a sweet deal—until you realize that for every booking the actor got, he or she went on hundreds of auditions and faced rejection over and over. By the time that commercial airs months later, the money is spent and the actor is looking for work again. Appearances aren't always what they seem.

Everyone I talk to on my show has reached a working level of success in their industry, and every one of them will tell you the same thing: don't get into this business for the money. It's the same reason you don't marry a guy for his abs: one day the abs will be gone, and you better love that guy or you won't stick with him. If your real dream is to be rich, there are much more effective ways to do it.

After I left the church, I've noted Katie and I discussed that I needed to at least try to be a performer. At the time I thought I would give it a go, and if it didn't work out I would be OK with moving on. Then something happened that changed my whole perspective: I realized that this is what I am supposed to do. My purpose is to bring people joy through entertainment. That means I have reached a point of no return. It isn't about fame or a paycheck for me. It is about knowing that I'm doing what I was designed to do.

Now if at some point I can no longer pay my bills by performing, I will take another job to feed my family . . . but I will never stop being a performer. My friend Christian is a very successful drummer and has toured with some of the biggest names in the business. He is a drummer because that's what and who he is. He has often referred to this phenomenon as a glorious curse. If you offered him a hundred thousand dollars a year to sit behind a desk or twenty thousand a year to sit behind a drum set, he would choose the drums every time. That is the power of passion.

Passion for what you do makes all the difference. It leads not only to greater personal satisfaction but it makes you more in tune with your fellow humans because you realize you are playing a part in the whole big picture. You are creating good in the world. I realize there are many people who are able to separate their purpose from their employment. They play vital roles in society doing their jobs well, and find their emotional rewards in other ways. I am very grateful for these people because we could not function as a society without them.

However, if you are one of the people who are driven by passion and purpose, if you can not separate what you do from who you are, there is a reason that fire burns inside you. Give yourself permission to do what you already know needs to be done. Share your art. Don't waste the talent that has been given to you for the hope that a good job will bring you more satisfaction. If there is one thing we have learned from situations like the 2008 market crash or the COVID-19 pandemic, it is this: ultimately, there is no job security. Any industry could be impacted by circumstances out of our control. If you want to live an *extra* ordinary life, you cannot settle for ordinary thinking. Safety is the enemy of creativity. Pursue passion over comfort and you will see what I mean.

Break the Rules

MANY OF MY favorite memories have to do with breaking the rules. When you are a kid, the list of things you shouldn't do is never-ending. For most of these activities there are even signs posted: No Skateboarding, No Loitering, and so on. The No Loitering sign always made me laugh because it means that you can't hang around somewhere without a purpose. That is the very definition of what it means to be a teenager. On Saturdays our entire agenda was basically loitering.

I know that ignorance of the law is not an excuse to break it—or at least I know that now. However, as a kid, if there wasn't a sign that said you couldn't do something, I considered these things open to interpretation. I was never a troublemaker, but I had plenty of times that I dipped my toe into the rule-breaking pond. The first time I ever did something like this it was with my parents. They were going to toilet paper their friends' house and brought us along. They didn't mention at the time that if you were caught you could be charged with littering, trespassing, disorderly conduct, or even criminal mischief. I figured it was because it was their friends' house and the friends would laugh it off it they got caught. So I made it a point to only TP the houses of people I knew.

One time my parents were teaching a Bible study at my friend Kyle's house, and a few of us kids were hanging out in the other room. Kyle's brother's friends had been mean to us earlier, so he had a great idea: he wanted to TP his own house and blame it on his brother's friends. We snuck out the window, and I felt the rush of rule-breaking as we covertly decorated their lawn with toilet paper. Who knew that Bible study could be the perfect alibi for semi-illegal activity? The best part is that no one ever found out we did this . . . I guess until now.

There was only one time that I broke my rule of toilet papering someone who wasn't a friend. What I am about to describe is incredibly reckless and dangerous. I do not recommend it, and it could have ended terribly. Side note: What is the statute of limitations on toilet paper crimes? OK, so here is what happened. When I was around eleven years old, I was hanging out at this same friend's house and there were some neighborhood high school kids that were super mean to him. Let's call their ringleader Todd. One day Kyle was walking home from school and it had just rained a ton. Todd drove up beside him in a black Mustang and splashed him with puddle water until he was soaked. The ringleader lived at the top of the hill that was around a very sharp corner by Kyle's house. If we were playing in Kyle's yard we could see Todd loading up his car with friends, and then about a minute later they would come flying around this sharp turn. Like, really fast.

We knew something needed to be done about this. Having been raised on '80s films, we assumed the only way to stop a bully from dangerous activity was to do a prank that was also highly dangerous. We got several rolls of toilet paper and stacked them on a broom handle, then taped the ends to Kyle's mailbox and waited for our opportunity. When we saw Todd and his high school gang start to load up in the car with his friends, we quickly ran back and forth, wrapping the TP from Kyle's mailbox to his neighbors' mailbox, effectively making a solid wall of toilet paper just after the sharp turn. About a minute later, Todd came flying around the corner, burst through the TP, and couldn't see a thing. He drifted back and forth as he screeched to a halt as his buddies screamed. We ran and hid the rest of the night so he wouldn't know it was us. We had just toilet-papered a moving car! I will never do it again but Todd also never sped around that corner again, either.

When I met my buddy Steve in high school, my level of questionable fun adventures went through the roof. One day Steve said, "Let's go to the movies." I told him I didn't have any money and he said *No problem, I have an idea.* By the way, this is the same Steve who thought the wheelchair firework stunt was a genius idea. We pulled up to the newest movie theater in the city. It was massive. Out front in the courtyard it had a huge fountain.

Steve went up to the ticket window and asked the employee, "If someone tossed a coin on the ground and walked away, who could have that coin?" They replied by saying, "Anyone who wanted to pick it up." Steve said thank you and then took off his shoes, rolled up his pants and climbed in the fountain to collect change. He then walked back to the same employee and paid for two movie tickets with the money. They gave us the tickets and my jaw hit the floor.

I mean, he kinda broke the rules, but he also got permission. The next time we went to movie they had a sign that said "Please Stay Out of the Fountain." We enjoyed the memory of that moment every time we visited the theater after that. When we were in college and had no money, we would spend entire evenings dumpster diving to find cool stuff. You wouldn't believe how much amazing stuff people throw away—and also a lot of gross things as well.

One of our biggest adventures was going with about twenty other college students to explore a place called Zelda's Cove. This was basically a storm drain about five feet in diameter that went under the city for about a quarter mile, and people decorated it like you would a haunted house. Through all these random acts of silliness I learned a couple valuable lessons. The first is that if your kids say they are gonna go hang out, get some clarification. The second and more important lesson is if you want to have extraordinary experiences, you need to do some things that are out of the ordinary.

Extra

I AM NOT encouraging criminal activity, but I am challenging you to think outside of the norm. There is a big difference in doing something because it is the right way to do it, versus doing it because that is the way it is always done. Life is not all laid out for us. The script has not been written so that we just have to follow the motions. This life is meant to be a Choose Your Own Adventure. While I have grown up a lot and have settled down a bit, I never want to grow out of chasing wonder. Remember that every day, no matter how dull it may seem, has the huge potential for adventure if your eyes are open to see it.

Make the Bread

As LONG AS I can remember, the idea of being a bread maker has been a goal of mine. Not as a career but as a hobby—a delicious, carb-consuming hobby. When I was a kid, one of the first trips I remember taking as a family was to San Francisco. I couldn't believe how great that city was and still is. Katie and I took a wonderful parachute trip there a few years ago, and I even took Maddy there for her ten-year-old adventure. (We told our kids that when they are ten, Dad would pick a place to take them on a trip, and when they turn sixteen, they could pick a place to go with Mom. Maddy is now fourteen and has already settled on going to Paris with Mom, so I hope this book does well.)

That first trip to the City by the Bay as a kid was completely wonderful. Riding the cable car, seeing the Golden Gate Bridge, it was all amazing . . . but the best part had to be the bread. The city is home to one of the most famous sourdough bakeries in the world. We took a tour of the factory and they showed us the process, which seemed very involved and a bit sacred. There is an element called the mother dough that acts as a starter for making bread. Each day you save a little bit of this dough and feed it to keep the starter going. So there is this natural yeast that grows and is passed on for years to come.

I had three takeaways from that experience: sourdough is delicious, I want to learn how to make it, it sounds too hard. The last one of those kept me from learning how for thirty years. There have been many times I didn't know how to do something, but I took the steps necessary to figure it out. For some reason, when it came to making sourdough I just assumed it was something I was incapable of doing. There was something blocking me mentally from being able to pursue it with intention.

When the first quarantine lockdown was ordered in California, I came to the harsh realization that all of my excuses for not learning something new or taking on a project were related to *time*. As I write this book we are still in limbo, not knowing what the outcome of this pandemic will be or when we will go back to anything similar to the previous life we lived. The one thing I know with certainty is that when this is over, no one will blame you for not taking action, but the excuse of not having time is no longer relevant. All we have is time . . . so I decided I would finally learn to make bread.

The first thing I did was text my buddy Andrew. He is a hilarious comedian; we have worked together a bunch of times at the Improv in Hollywood. He is what I call a bread guy. Meaning he not only makes bread, but he is passionate about it. I have since learned that breadmaking is something you don't really do unless you love it. There aren't a lot of people baking out of obligation. I just mentioned to Andrew that I was trying to find a starter for making sourdough. He immediately replied that he was at his in-laws in my city and could give me some of his starter.

Now it was on! Armed with Andrew's starter and a series of YouTube videos, I set off on a journey to make some bread . . . and on my first attempt, I totally failed. It did not work at all. The kitchen was a complete disaster. It looked like a science experiment had gone terribly wrong. Every surface was covered in dough and wet flour. I was tempted to buy into the old lie I had told myself—that this was beyond my abilities—but I pushed that aside and moved forward. I tried again after re-watching the videos and switching to a different flour, and it actually came out good. I was overjoyed, not just because I had made bread but because I had fulfilled a bucket-list item.

I now have a new hobby that I adore. The entire process of feeding the starter, making the leaven, folding the dough, and even waiting for it to rest has been a wonderful gift. The experience of making bread for me is rich with rewards. I find it soothing and incredibly tangible to be able to say, *Look what I made.* Also, we are in a season when putting bread on the table has been more challenging, pun intended. It is nice to see my family enjoy and gain sustenance from something I made myself.

Extra

THE DANGER WITH thinking something is too hard long enough is that you will replace that statement with saying it is too late. Every day there are success stories of people who started something new later in life. It may take you longer and the journey may be different, but *it is not too late*. We all have desires that have remained in the category of someday for longer than they should. Today is the day to get started—whether you want to write a book, learn an instrument, or just bake some bread (don't leave the oven on preheat). It is time to make the dough.

Your Big Break

I DON'T THINK that I am an overachiever, although I have been accused of being one. The reality is too many of us are waiting for an opportunity to arise. Waiting to be discovered. Waiting to have our big break. For much of my life, I lived the same way. I fell victim to the Hollywood success stories we have all heard. One day someone was just walking around the frozen food section at the grocery store and a talent scout plucked them from obscurity and said, "You're gonna be a star, kid!" That has happened to a total of three people in all of time. The success stories we see today are usually a product of a thought process that I like to call building your own platforms.

First of all, big breaks no longer exist in any industry. Take entertainment, for example. There used to only be three TV channels. If something happened on one of those channels, it was big time. Back in the '60s or '70s, if a comedian got a spot on the the *Tonight Show*, everyone would be talking about it at work the next day. You could become an overnight sensation just due to the sheer amount of focused attention on those networks. Today that is no longer the case. Between hundreds of cable TV networks, countless streaming services and social media networks, the supply of content is never-ending. Currently there are over three hundred hours of new footage being uploaded to YouTube every minute.

No one other than you is waking up today thinking about your career. If you want to make something, you are going to have to do it. This might sound discouraging, but I think it is actually the opposite. There have never been more resources available to build your dream than there are today. You just have to be willing to put in the time and energy it takes to learn, practice, and build your own platform.

When I was a kid playing in garage bands, we couldn't dream of recording our own music at studio quality—it would take thousands of dollars to pay an engineer with a proper studio to do the work. Today you can buy consumer-level gear that produces industry-standard audio and video and do it all from your own home. Many of the most successful entrepreneurs have realized you don't need massive warehouse buildings and hundreds of employees to build a dream. Jack Antonoff is one of the busiest producers in the music business (he recently coproduced Taylor Swift's album *Lover*). And he has made some of today's most recognized hits from inside his apartment; his unconventional way of creating has led to some incredibly unique sounds.

We live in a world where there are no gatekeepers anymore. If you have the talent, the dream, and the drive, no one can stop you from fulfilling your goals. The only thing stopping you from adding the extra in your ordinary is a shift of focus and mindset. Years ago, I became an avid podcast fan, and after listening to some of my favorites for months I thought, *I would love to be on a podcast*. So instead of wishing someone would invite me to theirs, I started my own on a whim. Did I know how to do it? No. I just committed to a start date, and then I had to do it. Over 150 amazing episodes later, I am so glad I took the leap and started.

One of my favorite comedy venues in Los Angeles used to be Meltdown Comics. This was where some of the most influential rising stars in comedy were performing. I wanted so badly to be able to perform on that stage. Then I realized I could wait around for someone to ask me to do five minutes on their show—or I could host my own show. Together with my buddy Eddie Furth, we launched *Jokers and Aces* (wow, I still love that name!). We would book our dream lineup of magicians and comedians each month, and when their fans came to see these insane shows, *we* were the hosts and fellow performers.

Extra

AS I WRITE this we are in a global pandemic that has all but annihilated the entertainment industry. No venues are open, no large events are being held, and most of the performers I know who were making a great living in the business are now on unemployment. The news media keeps referring to it as the "new normal," but I am again dreaming about how to have a little extra in my ordinary.

So while I write to you about building your own platform, I am sitting on a stage I have just built in my backyard. I plan to produce a series of social distance sideshows and put them out as a TV show. Will it work? I don't know. Is it a huge undertaking and a Hail Mary? Yes, it is, but just know I mean it when I tell you that *you have to build your own platform*. Lean in to wonder. Allow it to guide you. Look beyond the limitations and challenges you currently are presented with. There are 7.8 billion people who woke up this morning and the only one thinking about your dream is you. So let's go!

Epilogue

Life is not a puzzle to be solved, it is a mystery to be enjoyed. Keep chasing wonder

—Taylor, June 30, 2021
Upland, California

Acknowledgments

THANK YOU, MOM and Dad, for always pouring fuel on whatever sparks of interest I showed. I am so grateful to have family that I would choose as friends, and countless friends that have become family. This wouldn't have been possible without all of you.

About the Author

TAYLOR HUGHES FELL in love with the art of illusion when his parents bought him a magic kit for his seventh birthday. More than thirty years and three thousand shows later, Taylor has become known for his signature style of Magic Storytelling. He is a favorite at Hollywood's famed Magic Castle, a highly sought-after keynote presenter, and his special *Chasing Wonder* is currently available on multiple streaming platforms.

Taylor is married to his high school sweetheart, Katie, and they live in Southern California with their two daughters Madelyn and Kennedy.

CPSIA information can be obtained
at www.ICGtesting.com
Printed in the USA
LVHW030129150821
694943LV00004B/5